PSYCHOLOGY PRACTITIONER GUIDEBOOKS

EDITORS

Arnold P. Goldstein, Syracuse University
Leonard Krasner, Stanford University & SUNY at Stony Brook
Sol L. Garfield, Washington University in St. Louis

Pergamon Titles of Related Interest

Becker/Heimberg/Bellack SOCIAL SKILLS TRAINING TREATMENT FOR DEPRESSION

Carstensen/Edelstein HANDBOOK OF CLINICAL GERONTOLOGY

Fremouw/de Perczel/Ellis SUICIDE RISK: Assessment and Response Guidelines

Gotlib/Colby TREATMENT OF DEPRESSION: An Interpersonal Systems Approach

Matson TREATING DEPRESSION IN CHILDREN AND ADOLESCENTS

Saigh POSTTRAUMATIC STRESS DISORDER: A Behavioral Approach to Assessment and Treatment

White THE TROUBLED ADOLESCENT

Related Journal
(Free sample copies available upon request)

CLINICAL PSYCHOLOGY REVIEW

COUNSELING
THE BEREAVED

RICHARD A. DERSHIMER
Center For Living With Loss
Charlottesville, VA and Syracuse, NY

PERGAMON PRESS
Member of Maxwell Macmillan Pergamon Publishing Corporation
New York • Oxford • Beijing • Frankfurt
São Paulo • Sydney • Tokyo • Toronto

Pergamon Press Offices:

U.S.A.	Pergamon Press, Inc., Maxwell House, Fairview Park, Elmsford, New York 10523, U.S.A.
U.K.	Pergamon Press plc, Headington Hill Hall, Oxford OX3 0BW, England
PEOPLE'S REPUBLIC OF CHINA	Pergamon Press, 0909 China World Tower, No.1 Jian Guo Men Wai Avenue, Beijing 100004, People's Republic of China
FEDERAL REPUBLIC OF GERMANY	Pergamon Press GmbH, Hammerweg 6, D-6242 Kronberg, Federal Republic of Germany
BRAZIL	Pergamon Editora Ltda, Rua Eça de Queiros, 346, CEP 04011, Paraiso, São Paulo, Brazil
AUSTRALIA	Pergamon Press Australia Pty Ltd., P.O. Box 544, Potts Point, NSW 2011, Australia
JAPAN	Pergamon Press, 8th Floor, Matsuoka Central Building, 1-7-1 Nishishinjuku, Shinjuku-ku, Tokyo 160, Japan
CANADA	Pergamon Press Canada Ltd., Suite 271, 253 College Street, Toronto, Ontario M5T 1R5, Canada

---

Copyright © 1990 Pergamon Press, Inc.

Library of Congress Cataloging in Publication Data

Dershimer, Richard A.
    Counseling the bereaved / Richard A. Dershimer.
        p.   cm. -- (Psychology practitioners guidebooks)
    Includes bibliographical references.
    ISBN 0-08-036816-6 : --   ISBN 0-08-036815-8 (pbk.)
    1. Bereavement--Psychological aspects. 2. Counseling. 3. Grief.
I. Title. II. Series.
BF575.G7D47   1990
155.9'37--dc20   90-31383
                                                                          CIP

Printing: 1 2 3 4 5 6 7 8 9 10   Year: 0 1 2 3 4 5 6 7 8 9

Printed in the United States of America

The paper used in this publication meets the minimum requirements of American National Standard for Information Sciences -- Permanence of Paper for Printed Library Materials, ANSI Z39.48-1984

To those in the Caring Coalition Hospice
who demonstrated to me and hundreds of clients
and their families what loving, effective
bereavement care can be.

Contents

Preface

This book is for practitioners in the human and health services, those who serve the bereaved and others who would like to, including but not limited to therapists, counselors in diverse fields, social workers, physicians, and nurses. The chapters that follow present currently accepted approaches to bereavement care. Added, however, is a viewpoint based on principles of holistic care, typical to hospice work, that has not yet won widespread recognition in the behavioral sciences. This viewpoint assumes that grief is a natural process. Everyone suffers losses. It might be said that in addition to the two life certainties of death and taxes must be added a third—grief. It is how a person reacts to those losses that determines whether life will be lived well or poorly. Grief provides the opportunity for a person to discover individual traits that cannot be realized in any other way. The person can emerge with a greater confidence and deeper understanding of life in general, thereby better able to realize more of the potential he or she possesses; or let life's spirit ebb and his or her potential erode.

It is to this purpose of enhancing life that bereavement care should be dedicated—a fundamentally different approach than one based on "recovery." The recovery model begins with the assumption that grief either is a mishap that must be put right or an illness needing to be cured—nothing more. Recovery uses the scientific approach based on the delineation of clearly-stated goals, time frames, and treatment modalities, all intended to return the poorly-functioning person to normality as soon as possible.

Grief was not always regarded as unnatural. During my grandmother's days in England there was the saying: A woman isn't a real mother until she loses her first child. That phrase is more than an awareness of the high death rate among infants; it acknowledges the maturing experience of witnessing death. So, in a way, what is advocated in this book is a return to the beliefs of a previous age. However, today many people have to rely upon professionals to help them develop that awareness.

This book is written for practitioners by a fellow practitioner. To guide myself, I used the question, what did I want to know when I first began to help the bereaved? Often I used two companion questions: How was I helped when I was swamped by grief? In what ways could I have benefitted from assistance that I did not receive? The content that follows is shaped by research and scholarly thinking whenever possible but is supplemented and refined from 10 years of hospice work, and my own bereavement experiences. Most books written on the subject of grief are, I suspect, born of personal as well as professional encounters.

My interest in the field of bereavement resulted from an uncommon number of deaths of family members and friends during seven mid-adult years: a mother, two wives, and a good friend. My life was in shambles and I was left with three small children and two adolescents to care for and support. I did not want to return to my previous life-style and career. Through considerable hard work at individual, group, and self-therapy my psyche was repaired and a new life course charted. Little by little I also realized the influence and importance of my spiritual and religious beliefs. At the same time my professional interests shifted. I left professional education; first to prepare for family therapy with Murray Bowen, but in a few years I shifted to hospice work.

What fascinates me, as I review those changes, is how my interests— in psychological, spiritual, and career development—intertwined, each influencing the other. It is difficult now to separate my work from my personal life. I help bereaved clients, fellow church members, hospice staff, friends, and, on rare occasions (and most difficult of all), immediate members of the family. In return life has become more fulfilling, gratifying, mystifying, and fun than ever before—and I have not forgotten my own needs either.

The hospice field is a near-ideal location in which to develop my interests and ideas. Hospices are shaped by holistic ideals that foster attention to spiritual and religious matters along with physical and mental health care. Witnessing so many deaths and the consequent struggles of survivors to make sense of these events provides extremely valuable insights into how the human psyche and soul interact; insights that can feed self-reflection and growth. Hospices also are, at times, spiritual places, part religious institution and family as well as a health care agency. There are few organizations where such an awareness of individual needs, both among clients and staff, exists. I consider myself fortunate to be part of the hospice movement.

The idea of putting my insights into book form did not occur to me until Professor Goldstein, the editor of this series, suggested it. His current interest in bereavement care also came from personal experiences. I am deeply indebted to Dr. Goldstein for his support and guidance.

Others deserve special mention. My wife, Greta Morine-Dershimer, a consummate editor and tight-minded thinker, probably should be listed as coauthor for all the assistance she has provided. Mark Scrivani, a fellow trainer and reality-tester who advised me throughout, but especially on Part II of this book, is one of the few therapists to whom I refer the bereaved with confidence. Reverend Nick Cardell, my religious mentor, teacher, and minister of my church, helped to shape the message of this book over the years. Professors John Schneider and Ken Doka provided valuable support and the kind of expert consultation needed to keep personal views in touch with current thinking in the field. Elizabeth Corwin and her staff deserve plaudits for the very helpful editing. Needless to say, responsibility for the end product remains mine, alone.

Part I
Conceptual Development

Chapter 1

The Whys and Wherefores of This Book

Bereavement counseling. Grief therapy. Fifteen to twenty years ago these terms hardly appeared in the literature. As a professional, public service it was virtually unknown. Contrast that fact with the report in a July 22, 1989 newspaper that counseling had been provided in Sioux City, Iowa to the families of victims not yet identified from the crash of United Flight 232; clinical psychologists, some of whom had experience from previous flight disasters, had been flown in from Dallas as consultants and supervisors. Earlier that same year, Syracuse University organized campus-wide bereavement care for students affected by the loss of 33 of their peers in a plane explosion over Scotland. These are only two of many occasions when grieving victims were provided care by specially trained professionals.

Today it is not only during crisis situations that more care is shown to the grieving. Organized programs are offered by newly created hospices and bereavement organizations in existing community agencies such as child and family service centers, offices for the aging, regional Acquired Immunodeficiency Syndrome (AIDS) centers, and by schools and day-care facilities. The 1984 report of the National Academy of Medicine, *Bereavement: Reactions, Consequences, and Care,* (Osterweis, Soloman, & Green, 1984) describes a tremendous increase in efforts to assist the bereaved, citing, among other evidence, the growth in the number of support groups, the grass roots creation of hospices, and increased interest in books on the subjects of death, dying, and grief. Additional evidence includes:

1. the growing recognition in the professions that bereavement is a powerful, sometimes pathogenic event, both psychologically and physically;

3

2. a recognition that "normal" bereavement takes longer than previously thought; at least a year for most people;
3. the medical system's awareness of its impact on the circumstances surrounding death and its responsibility to the well-being of the family and others close to the dying person.

The report also cites an increase in demand for bereavement therapy and counseling that can be deduced from the growth in the number of bereavement therapists and counselors.

This growing interest in helping the bereaved reverses a previous trend. For several decades, Americans as a society displayed a baffling reluctance to acknowledge the seriousness of grief or to provide more than informal assistance to the sufferers. Item: Bereavement leave, as such, was unknown; after one or two days' absence from his or her job, the griever was expected to assume full work responsibilities. Item: Bereavement was not included among the human and health care services offered by community agencies. Item: Most of the public grief rituals, such as wearing black clothing and displaying crepe wreaths on doors disappeared, illustrating that individuals were expected to grieve in isolation. Item: We clung to the belief that except for extraordinary situations it was the individual's sole responsibility to pull through bereavement. It was widely maintained that if normal people exercised sufficient restraint and did not molycoddle themselves they would recover in a few short weeks or months. For those who experienced difficulties, family members, friends, the clergy, or family physicians could provide whatever support was necessary. Psychological practitioners were called on to help only in dire circumstances.

Why have these attitudes changed? One explanation is that as society's compassion for the dying increased, so did a sense of responsibility for those who grieve. Views held by health care professionals further reflect these changes. Hospices, for example, from their inception, have offered bereavement care to family members for a maximum of 13 months after the patient's death. Hospitals and other health care institutions now show more concern for the families of the dying.

ATTITUDES OF HUMAN SERVICE PROFESSIONALS

Health and human service professionals, psychiatrists, psychiatric nurses, social workers, and bereavement counselors, among others—increasingly aware of the interrelationship among the endocrine, central nervous, and immunological systems of the body—have been struck by the data revealing increases in physical and mental health problems among the bereaved. Mortality data show that widowers of almost all ages are at increased risk, especially within the 6 months following the death of a spouse. (Osterweis et al., 1984). These aspects of bereavement by themselves require greater professional attention.

Although this increased demand for bereavement support and care fills a societal need, it has placed professionals in something of a bind: The supply of services is not up to the demand. In no other professional field of preparation is bereavement identified as a separate specialty. (It is rare to even find an academic course so labeled.) As the National Academy report states, "family care following bereavement is still generally meager" (Osterweis et al., 1984, p. 216). They give three explanations for this discrepancy (p. 216):

1. inadequate preparation of professionals;
2. the stress that such care places on the staff, and the failure of institutions to acknowledge this fact through time and work-load adjustments;
3. the financial constraints imposed by third-party reimbursers.

Many professionals in the field of hospice care fully support the National Academy's observations and are far too aware of how few professionals understand the needs of those in grief.

Whatever the cause, the situation in bereavement care can be summarized as follows: A growing number of the bereaved have begun to seek help for themselves and their loved ones beyond the family and the traditional helpers—family physicians and clergy; this has led to a growing awareness that the complexity of bereavement requires special knowledge and skill in providing that assistance, however there are far too few professionals with this knowledge and skill.

WHY ISN'T THERE MORE AND BETTER CARE?

There are explanations for the present lack of counselors. Perhaps the most significant reason is that the knowledge base, on which all practicing professional fields are grounded, has been slow to evolve. Grief and bereavement as subjects were virtually ignored by the behavioral and social sciences until 15 to 20 years ago. The present state of knowledge reflects this immaturity. As we shall see in chapter 2 the leading researchers do not agree among themselves on many of the most basic matters—for example whether or not grief is, by itself, a unique human state separate from depression. This single issue has critical implications, of course, for professional treatment as well as for research. To regard grief as just one of many triggers for personality disturbances or other etiologies encourages the use of therapeutic practices designed for other diagnoses, which may complicate rather than facilitate the grieving process. To continue the example, many people experiencing acute grief display deep sadness, a state that appears to be an essential element in the bereavement process. These symptoms are often strikingly similar to clinical depression. However, to initiate treatment for the latter, either through medication or psychotherapy, might impede the grieving process.

Research in bereavement may never provide the knowledge base that undergirds other specialties in the behavioral and social sciences. Some workers in this field regard grief and bereavement, along with love, as the most powerful of all human reactions. Is it any wonder, then, that some of the most qualified authorities, such as Beverly Raphael, see research in this area making questionable headway?

To cite inadequate scientific knowledge as the only cause of the present deficiencies in bereavement care would be to ignore how most professionals use knowledge in practice. The "state of the art" from which they must draw is knowledge collected as much from their own and others' personal experiences as well as from research and scholarship (Schön, 1983). Professionals draw from a variety of sources in selective, highly individual ways, to devise personal theories and conceptual frameworks for their work. So it follows that, except for a few highly innovative practitioners, most professionals cannot exceed the limitations of the prevailing state in their respective specialties.

How is the quality of the state of the art measured? And can we say that it is deficient in the field of bereavement? This is not easy to ascertain. To look for fully developed theories or paradigms (Kuhn, 1962) is to encounter the more amorphous nature of most of the social and behavioral sciences, compared with the "hard" sciences. To seek consistency among recognized researchers is to overlook the richness of diversity during times of rapid advances of knowledge. To cite inconsistencies between practitioners' practices on the one hand, and recognized research evidence on the other, is to make a statement about the inadequacy of the networks through which knowledge is diffused, rather than about the state of the art itself. One measure cannot be overlooked, however, and that is the degree to which practitioners honor, or believe they must defer to and use, a discrete and recognized body of knowledge related to practice.

No competent therapist or counselor today would work with alcohol problems or sexual disorders without first becoming acquainted with the basic concepts and precepts of those specialties—even if special certification or licensing was not required. Why not? Because these specialties possess a number of well-defined treatments, more or less supported by theory and evaluation data, to claim membership in the specialty each practitioner must first master these treatments. Further, therapists without the specific knowledge necessary to accept certain cases—involving alcohol or sexual problems, for example—might be judged legally incompetent in litigation. There is not yet among the wider field of psychological practitioners the recognition that bereavement care possesses a discrete body of knowledge and set of treatments. Almost any practitioner may accept grieving clients—and then devise idiosyncratic practices to work with them.

HOW BEREAVEMENT CARE
CAN BE IMPROVED

Counseling standards must be changed. There are many valid research findings and much learned from practice—by volunteers as well as professionals—which must be taken into account by all practitioners who work with the grieving. There is no reason for the behavior of the bereaved to still puzzles many health-care professionals (Osterweis et al., 1984). That may have been the situation of the psychiatrist who accepted the mother of one of our hospice patients, a teenage, first-born son who had died of leukemia. After a few sessions she turned instead to a volunteer support group. "He wanted me to talk about my childhood, my career before marriage, my family relationships; I wanted to talk about Tony," she explained. The therapist should have known that the deeply bereaved need to talk about the deceased, endlessly and often monotonously; this behavior is not necessarily a sign of evasion or displacement of critical personality issues.

There are many useful, basic conclusions about the bereaved that must be understood if minimally effective practice is to be offered, such as:

1. bereavement is a process that changes over time (but time does not necessarily heal all wounds); reactions appear to be clustered into nonlinear phases;
2. depressive symptoms and emotional swings may last for at least several months and often for more than a year;
3. physical symptoms often appear in place of, or along side, psychological complaints;
4. some of the pain of loss can persist over a lifetime, without this being a sign of an abnormality.

The list is extensive, and grows. That is reason enough for a book like this—to help the psychological practitioner stay abreast of research and the reports of clinical work from which generalizations can be formed and reshaped. There is, however, another purpose.

Bereavement is a human response far more powerful and complex than is indicated by much of the research and other writings. In part this is because of the overemphasis on psychological variables. Freese (1977) maintains that too many writers view grief in fundamentally psychological terms. Some attention has been paid to the social and cultural implications. Much overlooked, however, have been the spiritual and religious dimensions of grief. The second purpose of this book is to continue to broaden the understanding of grief and bereavement by examining the religious and spiritual changes that can occur.

Psychology and psychiatry have had an uneasy relationship with matters of the spirit. Both have an unfortunate tradition to overcome, a past that stretches back in time to Freud himself. But even he, and many notable authorities since, felt the need to account for, if not to reconcile, the spiritual and religious with the psychological aspects of human existence. Jung and the depth psychologists, Frankl, Hillman, and Peck, to name but a few, have included matters of the soul, the meaning of life, and grace in their writings; their numbers may be growing today (see chapter 3). Peck (1978), for example, makes no distinction between the mind and the spirit, seeing spiritual growth and mental growth as one and the same. Dombeck & Karl (1987), too, see that spiritual matters are valid clinical issues; Kroll & Sheehan (1989), in their study of 52 psychiatric patients, concluded that religion deserves more attention in clinical practice and study.

We are concerned with the general relationship between psychology and religion mostly as background to more specific issues of grief and bereavement. For reasons that will be explored in greater depth in chapter 4, people who witness the death of someone they love can be confronted with some very basic issues of life. They may wonder what they did wrong to call forth death, or how they could have postponed the inevitable. Having failed to protect this beloved person, they wonder if any useful powers are still at their disposal. This can leave them feeling helpless, with the world consequently more threatening. As many survivors try to find some purpose in the life lost, they are confronted with the need to redefine their own terms of existence. To reduce these concerns to issues of guilt, lost relationships, and "goals for the future," as do some psychologists (social workers, nurses, doctors, and many others), is to miss the full richness not just of grief as a human experience, but of life itself.

To this author it is an axiom that humans, in addition to being psychological, social, economic, and political animals, also are inherently religious and spiritual. Therefore, to fully understand their responses to loss one must understand their religious and spiritual concerns. These are not limited to matters such as attendance at religious services, or membership in religious organizations, but include certain values, attitudes, and assumptions that are shaped and reshaped throughout life. These influence daily decisions and behaviors, but on certain occasions, such as in the selection of a mate or a job, they exercise greater influence than at other times. In bereavement, when basic personal matters are suddenly and dramatically questioned, the most fundamental religious and spiritual issues of a person's life come into play.

After the street murder of his wife, a rising young executive, who has believed he and his family have enjoyed the best life has to offer, is torn by the urge to leave everything and take his infant son to live as a common laborer in a protected rural environment. A middle-aged widow feels the pull to become more independent and in control of her life in ways that seemed impossible during her marriage. This questioning has been called a crisis in faith, or a turning point in life that could make everything different from then on.

This crisis can result in a full-scale reconstruction of an individual's religious and spiritual life. Some, then, will seek simplistic designs, precut models that fit any person and every situation. Others will find life transformed into something more marvelous and captivating, scary too, but challenging. The full seriousness of bereavement cannot be understood by researchers, practitioners, or the general public without a fuller appreciation of the changes that occur to the religious and spiritual lives of those experiencing loss.

Admittedly, this is a difficult statement for psychological practitioners to accept; most have little, if any, formal knowledge of religion and the spirit. The terms themselves are often misunderstood: Religion is thought of as allegiance to a recognized church, faith as the practice of its rituals, and the spirit as the essence of religious conversions. Even when there is a greater understanding of the issues, there is reluctance to pursue them in clinical practice. They are, after all, the purview of another specialist; it is consistent with modern-day professional care to refer clients with religious issues or problems to the clergy.

Psychological practitioners may have difficulty working with religious matters for another reason: Most therapists (Kroll & Sheehan, 1989) usually consider religious beliefs of clients to be symptoms of unhealthy behavior. Bergin's (1983) study of the psychiatric literature found a nonreligious bias, a limited appreciation of religious subcultures, and a conceptual and attitudinal bias that has prejudiced research findings.

Frequently, the first response clinicians have when encountering God-talk or religious points of view is to assess whether this behavior is the expression of a pathology. Even those psychologists and social workers who have become identified with secular humanism tend to deal with religion as a social institution and have few explicit ways of describing or dealing with spiritual experiences (Dombeck & Karl, 1987); the humanistic model of care seems more receptive to spiritual matters, but its secular bias makes it uncomfortable with God-language. Even those fields like psychiatric nursing and hospice care, which are sensitive to religious and spiritual matters, have difficulty preparing practitioners to recognize patients' spiritual needs.

Practitioners might be more aware of clients' religious concerns if they were more alert to the proper cues. Some wait for the broad philosophical question, the kind that touched off late-night college dormitory discussions, and overlook the simple, unembellished comments like, "I feel so helpless," or "What good are all these tests now, anyway?" The first question might properly be an indication of lowered self-esteem, but it also reflects a deeper sense of being adrift in the universe without purpose or direction. The second, in addition to indicating a need for explanations of medical matters, could reflect the crumbling of a belief in scientific medicine and the need for something to replace it.

Other cues can be missed because the client may use God-talk or speak in religious creeds. While this may be the only way many people can express certain religious concerns, it often is difficult for those outside these religious convictions to understand. Frequently heard are comments like "It's God's will," or "She's better off in heaven." I once asked a mother who had lost her 7–year–old daughter what she meant by saying, "God wanted her in heaven," and she replied, "My daughter will be protected by Jesus." From what, I wanted to know. The mother dodged the question the first time, and a few times thereafter. I suspected child abuse. Eventually, however, she talked about life's uncertainties and difficulties, and how she didn't want her daughter to grow up in a drug-infested, abortion-crazy world. It was better, she rationalized, that her child now lived in an orderly, secure environment, which the mother had felt totally incapable of providing for the daughter or for herself. The child's death, she finally was able to reveal, only intensified these feelings. These insights could have been lost in religious language and symbols.

It is difficult to determine when a client should be referred to a religious person. In the case cited above, the woman eventually chose to immerse herself in a new religion and found great solace and guidance from a responsible minister. At other times, when a client continues to use religious phraseology as a verbal shield or cliché, it probably would be best to refer her or him to a suitable religious leader, who can perhaps better understand the meanings behind the expressions and help the client to gain deeper insight into them. Keep in mind, however, the findings of Doka and Jendreski (1986) that show the clergy not well-prepared to work with grief. And clients may not always wish to be referred. As a nursing supervisor once said to a group of interns, "Honey, when one of the patients asks if you believe in God, he wants your opinion, not his minister's or rabbi's."

Be aware that there can be some unfortunate and unintended consequences of a decision to refer such a client: (a) a golden opportunity to fully explore significant issues may be passed up, and (b) the client may infer that these concerns somehow are not as important as psychological issues. Remember, also, that some 40% to 60% of the American people are not active participants in any formal religion, which means they probably do not have a comfortable, trusting link with a clergyperson. (For a further explanation of this point see Veroff, Kulka, and Douvan, 1981.) Many hospice family members, for example, prefer to deal with the staff pastoral-care person than with ministers, priests, or rabbis of the religious institution in which they claim membership.

Let us say that you, the reader, are convinced at this point that religious and spiritual dimensions of grief are more important than you had previously acknowledged. What do you do next? Engage in considerable study and thought. You may conclude that this is too much to undertake. And it would be if we came to the subject with a bare tablet. Fortunately, we do not—even those of us who have gone for years with little or no contact with established religions or theological thought.

If humans are religious and spiritual by nature, then we all cultivate these interests whether or not we are aware of it. This statement will be better understood after completing chapter 4. Suffice it to say at this point, as partial supporting evidence, that most of us find things that we regard as holy, commit ourselves to people or ideas that transcend immediacy, and try to find ways to link ourselves to life beyond this lifetime. We deal with these matters whether or not we participate in religious communities or become conversant with doctrines and catechisms. People who are not aware of their religious selves will be surprised (as was I) to learn how much they may have developed spiritually over the years without conscious attention. Consequently, undertaking a more systematic study of religion for adults becomes more like a graduate seminar than the undergraduate (or high school) course it first looked to be.

CLINICIANS MUST UNDERSTAND THEIR OWN BEHAVIOR

Practitioners can become more comfortable with and aware of clients' attitudes and behaviors during bereavement after they better understand their own responses to loss. It is gratifying to watch participants in grief workshops gain new insights about how they grieve. For most this is a novel experience, which is not surprising: Society has not encouraged us to talk with others or to think about grief; it is considered morbid, or as a group of sixth graders once said, "yucky stuff." Few have thought about what their bereavement behaviors accomplished—or failed to accomplish. They cannot identify the defenses they employed, and still use, in holding back the fear of personal death. These and a myriad of other unexamined matters hover in the dim recesses of consciousness like restless birds, easily flustered, threatening to become uncontrollable. In later chapters the reader can learn some ways of studying her or his grieving style—so the birds can be freed.

When professional therapists become more knowledgeable about their own bereavement behavior, as well as what has been learned from study and clinical experience, they can develop a different approach to working with clients. The awareness of bereavement as a natural process through which everyone passes at some point in life encourages therapists to become empathic, compassionate companions to the bereaved on this difficult journey. Osterweis et al. (1984) maintain that, like childbirth, bereavement is a process that can be helped by a professional, whether or not there are complications.

Birthing is a suitable metaphor in another way. Just as the arrival of a new child heralds the possibility of a richer, fuller life for the parents, so, too, can the loss of a vital relationship. Not at first, when grief is overwhelming and life is bare and seemingly hopeless, but later, as the griever regains the ability to be critically introspective and to appreciate light and darkness. It is then that the fullness of living, with its child-like sparkle, can be regenerated. Not for long, perhaps—some people may catch only faint glimpses of the possibilities before they dissolve like soap bubbles in the wind. The clinician's task is to help the bereaved have every possible opportunity to let that glimmer fire the imagination, so that each life can flower as never before.

SUMMARY

We need to redefine the nature and importance of grief and bereavement in the life process. It need not remain an event to be denied and ignored. If it is viewed instead as a time of opportunity for gaining insights about the human condition and a time to become rededicated to life's possibilities, what Schneider (1989, p. 27) calls the "transformative potential," then a more balanced view can emerge. This would allow the construct of bereavement care to become a way of helping people find spiritual reawakening, which may well be the way out of their pain.

The transformational power of grief is not a new finding. It can be found in historical as well as current religious, philosophical, and psychological literature. But it needs to be better understood, then more widely accepted, especially among psychological practitioners. It is important not only because it would help to shape their own work, but because professional therapists can play such important roles in helping the general public define conventional wisdom on a variety of topics. This book is designed to help clinicians better understand the part they may play in this task.

Chapter 2
Psychosocial Explanations of Grief and Bereavement

What have clinical studies and behavioral and social science research contributed as acceptable knowledge about grief and bereavement? These phenomonena have not been the subject of systematic research for very many years. In all of 1978 only 46 citations for "grief" were listed in that year's *Psychological Abstracts.* Over the next ten years interest increased remarkably; in 1988 there were 134 listings. Raphael and Middleton (1987) find that science literature in the field of death, dying, and bereavement has burgeoned in recent years.

STUDY OF GRIEF AND BEREAVEMENT

The rapid increase in the study of death, dying, and bereavement has led to weaknesses and confusion that are typical of most fields in their early stages of development. Schneider (1984) finds disagreement about the nature of grief. A special study of bereavement by the National Academy of Medicine (Osterweis et al., 1984) agrees, adding that there is substantially more concurrence about what constitutes pathology than there is about normality. Bowlby (1980) also finds the bulk of clinical literature concerned more with pathological variants of mourning than with the normal process.

Osterweis and coauthors find far more documentation in the literature from clinical records than from research, crediting epidemiologic research with providing more reliable data than experimental studies. Middleton and Raphael (1987) see that personalized, uncontrolled descriptions and case studies are common in the literature.

Excellent reviews of the literature have been provided by Raphael and Middleton (1987), Parkes (1987–1988), Osterweis et al. (1984), and Wortman and Silver (1989). While they indicate that there have been some valuable theoretical contributions, Raphael and Middleton (1987) see that most of the theoretical formulation have gone beyond the available data, with "hypotheses that may be untestable and concepts that seem incompatible with one another" (p. 5). They conclude that bereavement research is at an impasse and observe:

> Studies have not been able to provide systematic data which will allow any scientific statement about the *operational* criteria for defining a bereavement reaction and/or syndrome and whether or not this is "normal" or "pathological" in some way. Not only is there uncertainty in a scientific sense about such cross-sectional phenomena but also the processes of resolving and adapting to the loss have not been established in any broadly accepted framework, although psychoanalytic, behavioral, and other models have been proposed (p. 7).

The practitioner should not conclude from these assessments that there is nothing of value in the research literature. Rather she or he should be cautious in assessing what is read, especially when encountering universal statements.

Definitions

The existing research does not even make the task of defining terms to be easy. *Grief* and *bereavement* frequently are used interchangeably in the literature as well as in everyday useage. Nevertheless there appear to be some helpful distinctions.

Grief. Grief is used to describe the emotional pain that accompanies a sense of loss (Freud, 1961; Switzer, 1970; Freese, 1977). Carse (1981) finds grief to be a profound emotional crisis. Switzer (1970) observes that the concept of grief is used two ways in the literature: as if it were a separate emotion with its own unique set of chacteristics, without clearly differentiating how it is separate from other emotions; and as a complex combination of several different emotions, which are expressed at the time of death.

Several authors include more than affect in their definitions. Parkes and Weiss (1983) say it also is a process of awareness, of making real inside the self an event that already occurred in reality outside. To him grieving is a process of learning. Shuchter (1986) discusses the inter-relatedness of the emotional and mental responses. Schneider (1984) describes grief as a holistic process that affects people physically, emotionally, and spiritually.

Rosenblatt's (1983) data confirm the conclusions of Bowlby (1980) and many others that a variety of losses besides death can produce grief-like processes. Schneider points out that the loss of a relationship can be caused by marital separation, unemployment, relocation, or from growth into another developmental stage in life. Consequently, loss of an ideology or symbol, or of an object, place, or organization can result in grief. Simos (1979) sees that we grieve as young adults for the loss of youth and as a retiree for the loss of middle age. We can grieve for any cause to which we once gave allegiance. As Schneider (1984) notes, even successes like finding a mate, a job promotion, or inheriting large sums of money, produce changes that could require the giving up of a way of life, friendships, and a familiar life style. After the Loma Prieta earthquake, residents of the Bay Area reported psychological and psychosomatic symptoms that strangely resembled grief reactions. In short, any person or thing to which we form an attachment or, in the case of earthquake victims, something like the earth in which we place great trust and confidence, can be a source of grief when that attachment is broken.

Bereavement and Mourning. Some authorities define bereavement as the act of separation that results in grief, while others consider bereavement as a complex series of responses that follow a loss. Freese (1977) sees bereavement as the total sum of the behaviors that follow as a result of grief. Others limit its usage to situations involving a death (Raphael, 1983; Pollock, 1987).

Mourning is defined in traditional psychoanalytic theory as the necessary function of detaching the individual from the one (the object) who has been lost, whatever the cause of the loss. Uncomplicated mourning is defined in *The Diagnostic and Statistical Manual of Mental Disorders* 3rd edition, revised (DSM-III-R [American Psychiatric Association, 1987]) as a normal reaction to a significant loss, especially the death of a loved person. But Simos (1979) sees mourning as another ambiguous term, one that has been used interchangeably both with grief and bereavement.

Pollock (1987) extends the term, calling it mourning-liberation. He applies this term to all human response to losses, even those that occur from developmental changes throughout a person's lifetime, and suggests that all humans in every culture throughout history express mourning-liberation.

Operational Definitions in This Work. The consequence of this lack of agreement on basic terms is that for many years each author and researcher has had to redefine the basic terms in each document. Recently, however, there appears to be a convergence on definitions, which will be followed in this book. Grief has come to mean the complex, intense internal responses to all perceived and felt losses. The more someone has invested in a relationship, organization, ideology, location, or symbolic representation, the greater will be the distress and pain from the separation. Along with deep emotion there will be spiritual, psychological, and physical turmoil as well.

I agree with Lindemann's (1944) claim that grief is a natural response to loss. Like Parkes (1981), I view grief not as a state but as an emotionally-based process, changing its characteristics over time, and moving in irregular patterns from greater to lesser intensity. Initially the realization of the loss prompts shock responses, numbness, and a sense of unreality, or panic; sometimes these responses are intermingled with a person's reactions of detachment, denial, or avoidance. Shock reactions typically give way in a matter of hours or days to the distress and pain, pangs of intense or acute grief, the heartache of which so much poetry and fiction has been written. Over time these waves of pain occur less and less frequently even though they may never entirely cease, recurring on holidays and anniversaries, or whenever places, events, people, or objects remind the grieving person of what is missing.

Bereavement, as used in this work, describes the total recovery process of humans from the death of someone with whom they had a significant relationship. Bereavement includes much more than the pain of grief. It includes significant changes in the behavior, thoughts, attitudes, and in the religious and spiritual life of the bereaved. Relationships change; new friendships are formed with those who understand and are comfortable with grief; and existing friendships change in character and meaning.

No one is the same after experiencing the death of someone they loved; his or her life is refracted in some way, enriched by greater awareness and wisdom or blunted by fear and insecurity. Grief does not simply come and go. It must be dealt with, and because it is profoundly complicated, it calls upon individuals to make fundamental changes in their lives. That process is called "bereavement."

Different Conceptual Models

Just as definitions differ so do the theoretical models used by grief and bereavement researchers and scholars. Raphael (1983) identifies six models and their principal spokespersons:

1. psychodynamic model—Freud, Abraham, Fenichel, Loewald, J. H. Smith, Krupp, and Klein;
2. attachment model—Bowlby;
3. changes in the assumptive world, personal constructs, and cognitive models—Parkes, Woodfield and Viney, Horowitz;
4. stress models—Caplan, Maddison and Walker, Raphael;
5. illness and disease models—Lindemann, Engel;
6. sociobiological model—Averill.

The National Academy of Medicine report (Osterweis et al., 1984) uses five models: the psychoanalytic, psychodynamic, interpersonal, crisis, and cognitive and behavioral. It warns, however, that these several approaches do overlap, differing mostly in the emphasis placed on aspects of responses and in therapeutic techniques. The report documents agreement among the psychodynamic and cognitive and behavioral perspectives on two important phenomena: the emphasis placed on (a) the meanings attributed to the loss, and (b) the consequences to a person's self-concept. It also finds some additional agreement among the models concerning impulses and defenses that emerge during grieving and the impact bereavement has on people's belief systems and perceived locus of control.

Another way of understanding the different theoretical bases is through the metaphors various authors use. If you believe that bereavement is one of life's severe crises (Lindemann, 1944), the task of the sufferer can be viewed as having to "get through" a period of stress and confusion with as little damage as possible. Gerald Caplan, writing in the foreword of Glick, Weiss, and Parkes (1974), refers to bereavement as a period of transition, implying a passage from one life stage to another. Engel (1966) thought of grief as a sickness that needed to be cured.

These models and metaphors apply whether one is describing ordinary (normal) bereavement or dysfunctional (pathological) conditions. But the applicability of one over another may differ depending on which of the two conditions is being examined. Therefore it is helpful to look at the prevailing definitions for both ordinary and dysfunctional bereavement.

WHAT IS ORDINARY BEREAVEMENT?

The terms "ordinary" and "normal" should not disguise the tremendous variation in grief and bereavement reactions that occur from person to person. These can be attributed to personality variables and ethnic, cultural, and religious influences, as well as prevalent "myths" or conventional wisdom in any given group—the difficulty of generalizing about normal behavior is apparent. Nevertheless, there are patterns in bereavement that, by the frequency of their appearance, provide some sort of standard against which to assess individual bereavement reactions.

Phases of Bereavement

Almost all observers agree that bereavement is an active, evolving process. Some confusion arises in how to describe the process. It has become popular among authors of grief literature to cluster "characteristic" behavior at given points into stages or phases. Osterweis et al (1984) find that "most clinicians recognize phases of grieving" (p. 65). Raphael and Middleton (1987), however, remind us that there is little research evidence to support any pattern (or even the idea of a staged series). Nevertheless, the idea of having benchmarks is useful in illustrating the concept of movement through bereavement and in helping to better define the changes that occur.

Elizabeth Kubler-Ross (1969), originally more concerned with the processes of dying, is credited with having generated much of the interest in bereavement stages; her five stages of denial, anger, bargaining, depression, and acceptance have been used by many people to better understand more of the complexities of bereavement. Bowlby (1980) sees four phases of mourning:

1. the phase of "numbing" that usually lasts from a few hours to a week and may be interrupted by outbursts of extremely intense distress and/or anger;
2. the phase of yearning and searching for the lost figure, which can last for months, sometimes for years;
3. the phase of disorganization and despair;
4. the final phase, a greater or lesser degree of reorganization.

Worden (1982) uses four tasks of mourning: acceptance of the reality of the loss; experience of the pain of grief; adjustment to the environment in which the deceased is missing; withdrawal of emotional energy and reinvestment in other relationships. Parkes and Weiss (1983), revising an earlier description of four tasks to three, saw the first as the intellectual acceptance of the loss; the second as the emotional acceptance of the loss; and, finally, a change in the individual's model of self and outer world to match the new reality. Schneider (1984, 1989), too, has simplified his pattern. Originally he posed an elaborate holistic model across five dimensions (behavioral, physical, cognitive, emotional, and spiritual) that had five phases: initial awareness, holding on/letting go, awareness and gaining perspective, resolving, and reformulating. More recently he sees bereavement passing through three levels: discovering what is lost and coping with that condition, discovering what is left, and finding what is possible as a consequence. Shuchter (1986) describes six desirable tasks for the bereaved to achieve across three dimensions (changes in functioning, relationships, and identity):

1. learning to experience, express, and integrate painful affects;
2. finding the most adaptive means of modulating painful affects;
3. integrating the continuing relationship with the dead spouse;
4. maintaining health and continued functioning;
5. adapting successfully to altered relationships;
6. developing an integrated, healthy self-concept and a· stable world view.

Freese (1977) and Zisook, Devaul, & Click (1982) simplify the process by envisioning three stages: shock, the acute (or highly emotional) stage, and recovery or resolution.

I prefer the concept of phases and tasks of bereavement to that of stages, agreeing with Schneider (1984) that a "stage" implies incorrectly (a) particular behaviors occurring for a period of time, then disappearing as if resolved; and (b) one stage being more valued than another. The reader must be reminded that bereavement is far from being orderly; behavior described as characteristic of one period of time is likely to appear in all other phases even if not frequently or noticeably. Keep in mind, also, that not every person experiencing a loss may need to experience all these phases or accomplish all the tasks (Wortman & Silver, 1989). The phases I will use to demonstrate the characteristics and movement of bereavement for a grieving person are: reacting in shock to the awareness of a major loss; acute grief; the time of straightening up the mess; and reinvesting and reengaging in life. Each of these will be examined in greater detail.

Phase One: Shock. Sometimes referred to as the onset of the posttraumatic stress syndrome, this is the briefest of the phases, lasting a few days at most. An unexpected, sudden loss appears to intensify and prolong shock, but even persons who have had considerable advanced warning report being traumatized at the actual moment they became aware of the death. Reactions also may be amplified by unnatural causes such as suicide or homicide (Rynearson, 1987). Almost all observers of grief and bereavement concur that the news of a major loss is greeted by a mixture of disbelief, physical symptoms of shock, tension, apprehension, and anger, all of which can be mixed with a strange calm. Freese (1977) sees that this state of shock within minutes mercifully covers the cold, empty numbness and the confused, dazed feeling that follows the awareness of loss. Shuchter (1986) see this as the "wisdom of the body" used to protect us from emotional overload (p. 16). The tasks of this phase are to intellectually acknowledge the occurrence of the loss, to fully experience the jolting news, and to take the blow.

Phase Two: Acute Grief. Bowlby (1980) sees this phase beginning when the reality of the loss fully registers. Glick and coauthors (1974) believe it begins after the funeral or memorial ceremony is completed, for example, when the body is lowered into the grave. The prevalent belief among researchers and clinicians is that the acute grief phase is characterized by many emotional responses including pangs of intense pining, spasms of distress, restlessness, insomnia, preoccupation with the deceased, and anger. Being inundated with these emotional states, the acute griever is not only "poor company" but easily misinterprets interpersonal, social cues, which result in uncharacteristic behavior and errors of judgment. People occasionally experience near hallucinations like catching glimpses of the dead person in a crowd, misinterpreting a telephone voice as that of the deceased, or having dreams of the deceased that are so intense they appear real. Others claim to have had daytime visits where the dead one converses with them (Rosenblatt 1983, Glick et al., 1974). Rees (1971) documents the hallucinations of widows, finding that these experiences occurred more frequently than they were willing to admit to friends and family.

The acutely bereaved often worry about their own stability, and their preoccupation with the deceased may seem at times to be out of control. As painful as this phase is, the bereaved must endure. Bowlby (1980) writes:

> Only if he can tolerate the pining, the more or less conscious searching, the seemingly endless examination of how and why the loss occurred, and anger at anyone who might have been responsible, not sparing even the dead person, can he come gradually to recognize and accept that the loss is in truth permanent (p. 93).

The bereaved often are puzzled to discover that even though the loss has been accepted intellectually, they may continue to disbelieve its reality and seek the missing person's presence in the clothes hung in closets or stored in drawers. Glick and coauthors (1974) found that most widows did not fully accept their husband's absence. The bereaved may think they are being entirely rational when they continue to set a place at the dinner table or talk to the dead person when alone. Neither their judgment nor thinking can be fully trusted at this time, either in their business activities or their personal relationships (Freese, 1977). Lindemann (1944) finds that those he studied tended to increase emotional distance from other people. Furthermore, the risk of suicide is greatest during the first few weeks of bereavement, declining thereafter (Parkes, 1981). Lindemann, (1944) was the first to document the somatic distresses associated with acute grief, reactions such as a tightness in the throat, choking with shortness of breath, a lack of muscular power, an empty feeling in the abdomen, and intense distress. Raphael (1983) finds that some people express grief primarily in physical symptoms such as gastrointestinal disturbances, and the "vegetative" symptoms that, at another time, might signal the presence of a depressive disorder, that is, sleep disturbance, appetite disturbance, or loss of energy.

The period following the state of shock for some people may not, however, be characterized by high distress and depression-like symptoms. Wortman and Silver (1989) point to studies that identify people who do not exhibit these symptoms and who may not necessarily be denying or otherwise exhibiting pathological responses. Neither does it mean that they are not reacting in other, less apparent ways to their sense of loss.

How long will anyone experience acute grief? This depends on the

individual and the circumstances and meaning of the death. Vachon and
others (1982) point out that circumstances such as the griever's physical
health and financial status determine in part how long it takes to move
through this, and other, phases. Nevertheless, there is considerable agreement that the worst times typically do not last long; Raphael (1983) sees
the duration in terms of weeks or months. Glick and others (1974) found
that many of the young widows they studied had passed through the worst
symptoms in about 2 months after their husband's death. Margolis (1985)
found from his research that most grief counselors believed that acute grief
spans a period of only about 14 days. However, few of those who seriously
study the subject would disagree with Glick and coauthors (1974) that
some acute grief responses can be evident up to 3 or 4 years after loss
(Zisook et al., 1982; Margolis, 1985).

As with the shock phase, there is considerable individual time variation.
One way of explaining these differences is to think of the grief as continuing until a purpose has been served, until certain tasks have been accomplished. It is difficult to recognize when this has occurred, however, even
for the griever herself or himself. People often say months or years afterwards, "I thought I was doing so well back then, but now I recognize how
messy my life still was." Others who think grief is behind them find
emotions again erupting uncontrollably. As C. S. Lewis (1961) wrote, "For
in grief, nothing 'stays put.' One keeps on emerging from a phase, but it
always recurs. Round and round. Everything repeats" (p. 67).

Sooner or later, however, the times of pain and confusion appear less
and less frequently, and the preoccupation with the dead person decreases,
allowing difficult memories to sometimes become sources of comfort. The
griever is confronted with new awareness and motivation to tackle the
situation confronting him or her. It is this new awareness that leads to, and
is the hallmark of, the next phase of bereavement.

Phase Three: Straightening Up the Mess. Worden (1982) refers to this phase as
adjusting "to an environment in which the deceased is missing" (p. 14).
Schneider (1984) writes of gaining perspective on the loss, the time when
the pain is softened and replaced by a sweet sadness. People can look back
and discover the significance of what was lost. Glick and others (1974)
report that the widows they studied formed a new image and identity for
themselves that encouraged a return to social life after a few months. The
acute sense of loss changes at this time from a moment-to-moment preoccupation with the dead person to an episodic sadness evoked by special
circumstances.

As grief emotions tone down, bereaved people are able to find energy
and interest in tidying up their lives. But they are not yet ready to let go
of key features of the past system of which the missing person was a part.

A widower may adopt as best he can the mothering style of the missing wife, keeping the same daily routines, physical arrangements of the dwelling and customs during holidays. In another family, the children may be expected to share in the missing father's tasks, with the oldest son being asked to assume some of the fathering of younger children. Keeping the old system going as much as possible provides the security of a familiar, if altered, life-style and buys time for the bereaved to gain the necessary intellectual perspective and emotional "breathing space" for continued healing.

It could be argued that this is not the old system that is being preserved but a new one or, at least, a system in transition. Whether this is true or not, for a while the bereaved may attempt to preserve as much of their past life as they can. For some of the bereaved, like elderly people with limited financial or physical resources, this is a wise and realistic conclusion that will last for the remainder of their lives. As one 72-year-old woman once explained, "I had this man, a dear friend, talk to me about marriage, but I couldn't see it. All those adjustments again. (Sigh.) Just too damn much trouble."

The major task of this phase is for the bereaved to take stock of what is left in their lives. One word summarizes what needs to be done: assessment. They must work out new relationships with family members and friends. They must inventory their finances and other resources. Basic assumptions about their lives, their world, and the source of divine inspiration and commitment must be examined. They must determine what remains in their lives.

Phase Four: Reinvesting and Reengaging in Life. There are many different terms used to describe the final phase of bereavement—recovery, adjustment, and completion are among the most common. Each of these, however, implies some unfortunate connotations. "Recovery" carries medical overtones as if an illness had been overcome. "Adjustment" indicates the bereaved are making the best of an unpleasant situation. "Completion" suggests that grieving is at an end.

There are other descriptions. Worden (1982) uses the phrase, "to withdraw emotional energy and reinvest in another relationship" (p. 15). Parkes and Weiss (1983) speak of a new identity, a new set of assumptions about one's own self. But it is Shuchter's (1986) concept of the emergence of a new personal identity that this author most favors. To Shuchter bereavement can provide new and deeper insights into the way one perceives the self in relation to the wider world.

Shuchter goes on to say about his subjects, "By the end of 2 years of bereavement, the majority of widows and widowers are able to regard their grief as a growth-promoting experience, and their self-images as primarily

positive" (1986, p. 272). Glick and coauthors (1974) found in their study
of the bereaved that recovery included:

1. more control of their lives;
2. fewer tears;
3. fadings of feelings of abandonment;
4. a personal sense of recovery and higher energy levels;
5. a growing interest in activities and being with others;
6. times of peace;
7. less often seeking advice from others;
8. a new sense of respect for self and confidence in ability to cope;
9. less fear of being alone.

The bereaved that Shuchter (1986) interviewed go on to mention many
similar qualities, like developing greater confidence, autonomy, freedom,
assertiveness, and openess. Some found themselves to be more spiritual,
sensitive, and compassionate. Schneider (1984) writes of people transforming loss into new levels of attachment and gaining a new sense of the
meaning of life from the experience.

Clearly these changes indicate that more than just a recovery has occurred. Reengaging in life offers the opportunity for a restart, with greater
intensity and deeper insights into life's journey toward greater individuation of self. Those opportunities are far from guaranteed, however. The
person reaching this phase is faced with a critical choice: reinvesting in new
relationships, helping to fashion new human systems, reconstructing more
nourishing religious views, and regenerating spiritual drive; or viewing
himself or herself as handicapped in some way, unable from that time
forward to take advantage of all that life has to offer. I shall elaborate on
these alternatives in later chapters.

What Affects the Process?

As stated previously, no two persons will pass through the changes
described above in the same way. Many factors help to explain these
differences. The 11 that are selected do not exhaust the list, but each is
supported by much discussion in the literature and help to demonstrate the
range and complexity of bereavement. These 11 are:

1. personality variables;
2. past grief events;
3. complexity of each bereavement situation;
4. developmental factors;
5. anxiety about death;
6. extent and quality of social supports;

7. ethnic and cultural influences;
8. type of death;
9. gender;
10. quality of the lost relationship;
11. spiritual and religious outlook;

These shall be discussed in order.

1. Personality Variables. There should be no doubt that personality variables affect bereavement as they do all other aspects of behavior. The way a person responds to stress and anxiety will determine in many ways how she or he will handle grief. Especially important are the defenses employed that lead to avoidance, denial, or postponement of grieving.

Simos (1979) sees that denial is the foremost defense in bereavement, shutting out of awareness aspects of reality needed to process grief. According to psychoanalytic theory, denial is an unconscious defense used to reduce, avoid, or prevent anxiety that arises from an objective danger. It is a normal part of ego development, useful during difficult times in order to make life bearable.

Bowlby (1980) employs an information-processing model to explain the concept of defenses. He maintains that certain types of unpleasant or threatening information will not be processed internally for relatively long periods of time, sometimes permanently. The more completely a person's attention, time, and energy are concentrated on defenses the less energy is available for constructive interaction with other aspects of reality. The bereaved pay a high price for shutting out the stimuli that produce pain and suffering; eventually denial can hinder the development of further emotional attachments, not just to someone like the deceased, but in all relationships.

2. Past Grief Events. The number and impact of previous losses and the degree of resolution of past bereavements impact on and help to shape responses to additional losses. It is difficult if not impossible to ascertain for any one person the degree of resolution of previous bereavements. If grieving for all major losses is never fully completed (Bowlby, 1980; Osterweis et al., 1984), leftover emotions are likely to surface with each recurring loss. Raphael (1983) sees that many losses that at first appeared to be insignificant may reappear with a new grief. Major losses, Schneider (1984) reminds us, or serial losses within a relatively brief period of time, can both prolong bereavement adjustment and intensify grief.

It would seem to follow that the older a person is, the more leftover grief accumulates. This should lead the elderly at some point to be overwhelmed by recurrent losses. Some are. But Kalish and Reynolds (1981) find the elderly they studied were more relaxed about grief and mourning than many younger respondents. The researchers speculated that accumulated bereavement experiences can also provide a perspective and balance in people's lives.

3. Complexity of Each Bereavement Situation. Many reactions to a loss are complicated by (a) the severity of that loss, and (b) the many other changes that occur as a consequence. Intuitive good sense supports the conclusion that the length and magnitude of grief reactions are related to the severity of the loss, however that severity is determined by the individual. The number and complexity of the concomitant changes occurring as a result of a loss also affect bereavement reactions (Middleton & Raphael, 1987).

What are some of these complications? A short list includes dysfunctional behavior by other members of the family, financial problems, marital separation, the recurrence of previously dysfunctional behavior, and the disintegration of social support networks. Bowen (1976) sees emotional shock waves that reverberate throughout the family system for years following a major loss. These cause individuals to respond in ways that can further complicate family functioning; the teenage son, his life made more uncertain by his father's death, acting on impulses to feel adult and in control, "falls in love" and hastily marries an older woman with a child; this causes the mother, feeling she has failed as parent, to become more harsh and restrictive with the other children, which, in turn, causes the next oldest son to become more rebellious—and on it goes. The shock waves, Bowen claims, can last for years, beyond the usual time most people allow for bereavement.

4. Developmental Factors. Is the impact of a major loss greater at certain times in our lives than at others? The conclusions are far from clear, but there is some intriguing evidence and speculation. If children are more vulnerable to long-term impact than adults, as some believe, it probably is because of their insufficiently developed coping capacities (Osterweis et al., 1984). Silverman and Silverman (1975) agree that children are especially vulnerable, however, they warn that this may be attributed to many factors: the impact of the death on the total family; the availability and effectiveness of the parent substitute; and the developmental level of the child, especially his or her understanding of death.

Jaques (1973) writes of the heightened awareness of death at critical change points or "crises" in adult development, especially during the so-called mid-life crisis—typically the time when humans reshape their images of mortality. Another redefinition of life in general usually occurs at full maturity, around the mid-sixties. Women may be triggered to review their lives around the onset of menopause, not only due to the changes that occur to their bodies, but also because of the psychological sequelae that accompany these physical changes.

The life cycle can be divided into a sequence of four eras for men: childhood and adolescence; early adulthood; middle adulthood; late adulthood (Levinson, Darrow, Klein, Levinson, & McKee, 1978). These are times of relative unity and stability when a man's values, image of and esteem for the self, personal goals, key relationships, and many other factors have consistency and some clarity. The transition from one era to the next is, by comparison, a time of change and insecurity. Sheehy (1974) saw some parallels in female development.

Much more study is needed of the influences on bereavement of developmental factors for both men and women. It seems entirely possible, however, that reactions to loss could be intensified during the uneven times of transition.

5. Anxiety About Death. It is generally believed that fear of death can play an important part in shaping grief reactions but no one seems particularly sure of just how. Fear and anxiety remain complex human responses. This is due in part to the fact that fear of death is not a single unified concept (Raphael, 1983). To most people it is essentially an unknown state that has "multiple meanings and images projected onto it," such as "abandonment, and violence directed at the helpless individual" (Switzer, 1970, p. 326). There can be anxiety about death in persons for whom there is no immediate or known menace to life, whose physical health is excellent. Death could represent the unknown, terrifying force over which humans have no control. Or it could represent what Jaques (1973) describes as the "misery and despair of suffering and chaos unconsciously brought about by oneself" (p. 147).

In spite of this confusion, and perhaps because of it, people attempting to understand their own or another person's bereavement must develop some awareness of the fear of death that may have been triggered. It makes sense that the confrontation of another person's demise can evoke thoughts, images, and feelings within the survivor—because death awaits us all. Mental health workers should especially take note that their own existential anxiety can be aroused when serving the grieving (Worden, 1982).

6. Extent and Quality of Social Supports. Few question the conclusion that those in bereavement benefit from having friends and/or family members to whom they can turn for assistance and empathy. Vachon and others (1982) find that isolation and the lack of social support was the most common ingredient among bereaved women who were still enduring high distress 2 years after a death. Purisman and Maoz (1977) report that family adjustment after the loss of sons in war was significantly related to past and present interpersonal relationships.

Osterweis and coauthors (1984) warn, however, that the concept of social support can be misleading in two ways: during the grief crisis an otherwise stable and reliable interpersonal scaffolding can become shaky because of the loss of a key member; and too often the term "support" is interpreted to mean just attention to emotional needs. The bereaved also need:

- logisitical assistance (babysitting, household management, financial management, and the like);
- helpful information and knowledge about the general impact of grief (what is considered to be typical grieving, "how to" information for better personal and family functioning, etc.);
- opportunities to reflect on and benefit from religious and spiritual beliefs;
- reaffirmation of significant and comforting values and beliefs;
- reflection on and reaffirmation of shared norms that provide meaning;
- empowerment of abilities so as to become more self-reliant at critical times;
- encouragement to express emotions.

Most of the widows studied by Glick and associates (1974) reported that after the death a new cast of helpers appeared to replace the predeath supportive community. Some friends and relatives are better at offering emotional support during acute grieving, while others better facilitate adjustments during later stages. A support network that may be optimally helpful at one point in time may be dysfunctional at another time (Glick et al., 1974). Raphael (1983) points out that it is not just the availability of friends and family members that is important but how helpful the griever perceives them to be.

Family supports are regarded in the same way. Glick and others (1974) find that bereavement brought most widows closer to their own families, although, as with friendship networks, there were changes over time in both the intensity and focus of those relationships. Again, it was the quality, not just the availability, of family support that was critical. There is evidence that most of the families having problems in bereavement had them before the death tragedy (Purisman & Maoz, 1977).

Certain practices and mores of ethnic and religious groups provide supports in times of bereavement. These include such help as having women from extended families and/or neighbors assist in the running of households and watching children.

7. Ethnic and Cultural Influences. Kalish and Reynolds (1981) studied the reactions of four different ethnic groups (Anglo-Americans, Black-Americans, Japanese-Americans, and Mexican-Americans) to the death of a family member. They identified a variety of cultural and ethnic influences on the way a loss is perceived and experienced. For example, they found that Japanese- and Mexican-Americans more than the other two groups tend to seek support from family members. Osterweis et al. (1984) point out that certain ethnic groups—southeast Asians for example—do not like funeral directors to handle the dead and do not use health professionals for counseling. It is common knowledge that some cultures foster public manifestations of distress while others inhibit public display.

Osterweis et al., (1984) reviewing the influence of culture and ethnic identity on the way loss is perceived and experienced, conclude that mainstream, middle-class Americans are affected by the tradition of individualism, the social arrangements of close nuclear families, loose social networks, and the weakening of traditional, sacred, and secular bereavement rituals. Raphael (1983) concludes that many of the ceremonies and rituals of other cultures better serve the emotional needs of the bereaved than do those of modern Western society.

8. Type of Death. Are certain kinds of deaths more difficult for the survivors than others? Conventional wisdom supports that contention: for example, suicides, accidental and other sudden deaths, and the deaths of small children are deemed more stressful in general than deaths of the elderly. Suicides are of special significance (Raphael, 1983). Farberow, Gallagher, Gilenski, and Thompson (1987) studied 108 survivors of suicides and found poorer mental health on all measures compared with the two control groups. Peach and Klass (1987) report that the parents of murdered children felt overwhelmed by their experiences. Osterweis and associates (1984) cite evidence that shows marital discord or divorce in 50% to 70% of families that lose a child from cancer. Generalizations from these isolated studies, however, are not easy to support.

Osterweis et al. (1984) write, "contrary to commonly held views, most of the research literature indicates that sudden death, however defined, does not produce more disturbed survivors" (p. 38). And while Middleton and Raphael (1987) agree that the severity of the loss is related to the length and magnitude of grief reactions that follow, they emphasize that severity is determined by the individual: the natural death of a 90-year-old can be just as disturbing to one person as the suicide of a teenager is to another.

9. Gender. Do men and women grieve differently? The evidence is far from exhaustive. Silverman (1981) concludes that grieving women more often than men are in a precarious relationship to the larger community to which they relate, and women's sense of self, being reflected more in their relationships with others, is more threatened by losses. Glick and associates (1974) found many similarities in the behavior of the widows and widowers they studied but also several important differences:

1. men tended to interpret their losses in terms of dismemberment while women used terms connoting abandonment;
2. men found it more difficult to give attention and energy to their work after the death whereas women tended to find solace in work;
3. men much more than women were unable to display their grief and, as the year of bereavement progressed, men ended emotional display more quickly than women;
4. fewer men than women blamed fate or became angry with those who had not had similar misfortunes;
5. men exhibited less guilt than women as time went on;
6. men remarried more quickly and, in general, moved more quickly toward social recovery than women;
7. men cared more about maintaining their highest levels of functioning, and were more dismayed than women by the loss of energy and competence;
8. the lack of a sexual partner was more bothersome to men than women;
9. despite the more rapid movement of men toward social recovery, their movement toward emotional recovery was slower than that of women.

It must be remembered that these findings, while interesting, were based on a sample of 43 women and 16 men. In another small-sample study, Purisman and Maoz (1977) found no significant differences in the responses of male and female parents to losses of adult children in war.

10. Quality of the Lost Relationship. Conventional wisdom concludes that the more emotionally involved a relationship is, the greater will be the feelings of loss at its termination. Prior dependency of the survivor on the deceased, for example, appears to lead to difficulties in bereavement (Parkes & Weiss, 1983; Horowitz et al., 1984). Also, the survivor whose spouse was their lover and only close companion should find their life more askew than a person who had many outside interests and friends. It would seem to follow that a person who felt ambivalence at the time of a spouse's death would be relatively detached from grief. But ambivalency toward the former partner often intensifies and complicates bereavement (Parkes & Weiss, 1983; Rynearson, 1987; Marris, 1974). The quality of a relationship at any given point is difficult to determine. It becomes complicated during bereavement when the deceased tends to be idolized.

11. Spiritual and Religious Outlook. How do religious beliefs and practices influence the intensity and characteristics of grief? Evidence from behavioral sciences research is not easy to locate. The 1984 National Academy of Medicine report (Osterweis et al., 1984) has few references, out of several hundred, that address spiritual or religious issues. That lack may be explained by Larson (1986) who reveals that only 59 out of 2,348 research articles on a variety of topics (not just bereavement) in four psychiatric journals during the years 1978 to 1982 included a quantified religious variable. Most often in those 59 articles, the one variable studied was a single, static measure of religion, such as frequency of church attendance, rather than multiple, dynamic measures. He finds more conceptual and methodological sophistication in psychological and sociological studies but concludes, overall, that religion is largely overlooked by the behavioral and social sciences. This is further evidence of the separation between the sciences and religion, cited in chapter 1, which will be dealt with in more detail in following chapters.

DYSFUNCTIONAL OR PATHOLOGICAL BEREAVEMENT

"My mother sits home alone day after day. All she does is watch television or read in between visits to Dad's grave, two, three times a week. That's what she seems to live for—those visits when she kneels down and talks to him—as if he were there, listening. Once in a while she'll go to a movie with us, or for a drive. Or let a friend come visit. But not often. I don't know. Is she losing it?"

Questions like that are frequently asked by clients or participants in workshops on grief. Or the bereaved themselves will describe their behavior and ask, "Am I going crazy?" A friend who led a young widows' support group for more than 3 years reports that, at some point, without exception, every one of the several dozen women who attended admitted doubts about their sanity.

Insanity can be suspected because the bereaved's behavior will be so changed and so uncontrollable. Tears flow with seemingly little provocation, thoughts wander at will, there is so little interest in activities or people, and too little energy. And after a few weeks, when so many people mistakenly believe that bereavement should have long since subsided, things may remain as bad as ever.

This confusion over ordinary grief only complicates the difficulties of determining when the process goes awry. How often does this occur? Figures are difficult to find, but three studies indicate that from 12% to 15% of the bereaved have exhibited intense and prolonged reactions, indicating pathological tendencies (Clayton, Desmarais, & Winokur, 1968; Zisook et al., 1982; Parkes and Weiss, 1983).

There are many different labels for extraordinary grief. Parkes and Weiss (1983) speak of prolonged or chronic grief. Osterweis et al. (1984) use the term pathological grief, as does Worden (1982) who also speaks of abnormal grief reactions and complicated mourning. Freese (1977) acknowledges the applicability of all these terms and adds other adjectives (uncompleted, ineffective, complicated, inhibited, delayed, and prolonged) to the list.

These many labels reflect the difficulties of diagnosing bereavement that does not proceed as expected. Freud (1961) recognizes that profound mourning and melancholia were not easily differentiated one from the other. Osterweis and associates (1984) point out that what constitutes too much or too little grief in terms of psychological well-being has not been definitely determined by empirical research. Middleton and Raphael (1987) see that while concepts such as chronic, delayed, and distorted are widely used, their validity has yet to be established. Simos (1979) writes that grief involves such profound changes that its symptoms often resemble those found in physical, mental, and emotional disorders; for example, the display of strong feelings can be misinterpreted as a sign of psychosis. She also warns that some unpleasant outcomes, for example, despair, may be realistic given certain circumstances.

Whether or not there is a growing consensus on psychological pathologies of grief, many findings and observations bear attention. Parkes and Weiss (1983) write, "there are grounds for regarding pathological forms of grief as separate conditions in their own right, having distinctive etiology, psychopathology, symptomatology, and prognosis" (p. 9). They claim that most observers see two major groups of factors that can complicate responses: those that prevent the expression of grief, usually at the onset; and those that delay or prevent its termination. Bowlby (1980) sees two main variants: the prolonged absence of conscious grieving and chronic mourning. Raphael (1983) agrees with those categories and adds one she calls distorted bereavement—marked by intense, pervasive anger and overwhelming guilt. Lindemann (1944) found the most frequent distortions of grief to be its delay or postponement. Brown and Stoudemier (1983) use five classifications: (a) when grief manifestations are absent (b) when they are of extreme intensity, (c) when they are prolonged, (d) when they develop into a major depression, and (e) when they become distorted. Osterweis and associates (1984) use three: prolonged or chronic grief, the absence of grief, and delayed grief.

There are objections to these conclusions. Wortman and Silver (1989) cite evidence that refutes "the assumption of intense universal distress following a major loss" (p. 350), which raises doubts about whether the absence of grief can be labeled "abnormal." Rynearson (1987) questions the definitions of pathological grief that are based on distortions of normal grieving, when "normal" remains such an elusive term. He emphasizes the tremendous variability of responses including little or no apparent reaction to loss. As replacement he has developed a three-part typology of pathologic grief:

1. dependent grief syndrome—clinging or overreliant attachment;
2. unexpected loss syndrome—avoidance leading to chronic anxious withdrawal;
3. conflicted grief syndrome—ambivalent attachment leading to delayed responses.

Regardless of those objections, the practitioner cannot ignore the most generally accepted thinking about distorted bereavement. For that reason I shall provide a summary using the three categories of dysfunctional bereavement that appear in the preponderance of the literature: prolonged or chronic grief, the absence or delay of grief, and exaggerated expressions or forms of grief. These should be used as a way of remaining alert to clues that can increase the clinician's awareness of the bereaved's state and progress rather than as diagnostic categories.

Prolonged or Chronic Grief

The studies of Parkes and Weiss (1983) and Vachon and associates (1982) find that prolonged and persistently severe grieving without diminution in intensity over time is the most common form of pathological grief. Freese (1977) agrees, noting that when the grief work is not carried to completion, the bereaved person is left with many problems that can surface in a variety of ways. Raphael (1983) cites as an example the man who, 3 years after his wife's death, remained angry and resentful at the world, visited her grave twice a week, and refused to take care of himself properly. Osterweis and associates (1984) see chronic grief as caused by the bereaved actively resisting movement through the process.

Grief can be prolonged by external circumstances beyond the griever's control, however. For example, Peach and Klass (1987) find that the parents of murdered children were unable to resolve their grief until legal processes had been completed. Doka (1986) explains that bereavement is prolonged because society will not recognize certain people's right to grieve, including exspouses, cohabiting but unmarried couples, friends of AIDS victims, and women who had abortions; he calls this disenfranchised grief. People in these circumstances should not be considered as experiencing a pathological state.

Absent or Delayed Grief

The absence of grief is viewed as more serious than delayed grief. It is not a common condition (Parkes & Weiss, 1983) but it does occur. Bowlby (1969) writes of people who appear to the casual observer to be carrying on as if nothing has happened. Lifton's (1979, 1982) studies provide a possible explanation of this phenomenon. After interviewing about 75 survivors in Hiroshima, he found people with a diminished capacity to feel, a condition he terms psychic numbing. It is a defense mechanism, a radical disassociation of the mind from its own forms, which at first enables survivors to cope with experiences and images otherwise too threatening and overwhelming to their sanity. But when this condition persists, the mind itself eventually becomes deadened, awareness becoming severed from emotion, knowledge from feeling. Lifton maintains that many of these patterns that were seen to occur both in victims of Hiroshima and German death camps can occur to others in "ordinary" death encounters, such as losing a beloved person.

Not all people who delay grieving, or who show few grief symptoms, however, can be considered pathological. Horowitz and associates (1984) point out that some defenses like the temporary absence of grief serve the purpose of letting into the consciousness at any time only the amount of reality that the ego can safely handle. Some people must postpone grieving because of circumstances that demand priority attention and resources, such as women who are near to giving birth, widows or widowers with small children who must survive economic hardship, and others who are physically injured. In some circumstances it may be possible to put off grief until more suitable times without the griever becoming impaired (Wortman & Silver, 1989). Raphael and Middleton (1987) reminds us that some bereaved appear to recover satisfactorily without experiencing a major bereavement reaction. Nevertheless, there is considerable agreement among others, including Raphael, that a prolonged delay of the onset of grieving, for other than obvious reasons, is usually a harbinger of difficult bereavement. Some researchers see this to be the onset of a new affective disorder episode (Osterweis et al., 1984).

Raphael (1983) differentiates between delayed and inhibited grief, the latter occurring when the expression of grief is turned off or turned down. Inhibited grief not only stifles the emotions, it prevents the review of the missing relationship. Raphael, Bowlby (1980), and Parkes (1980) all see this review as essential to the grief process.

Ethnic groups can influence the timing and expression of grief. Freese (1977) points out that all too often in our society the seemingly all-American mourner who conforms to expectations and steadfastly stands resolute, denying the seriousness of the loss, may find his personality affected in baffling ways.

Exaggerated Expressions of Grief

There have been many attempts to identify the exaggerated expressions of grief that predict abnormal bereavement. Lindemann's (1944) study became a landmark, identifying nine distortions, including factors such as:

overactivity without a sense of loss, engagement in activities detrimental to one's own social and economic existence, and alterations in relationships with friends and relatives. But in what combination any of these nine factors must appear, and under which circumstances, have never been reliably determined.

Raphael (1983) reports that several different studies have identified patterns of symptoms that appear following the death of a spouse. These include depressive moods; neurotic disorders such as phobias, obsessions, hypochondriasis, conversion reactions; and illnesses. She reports that certain other bereavement responses have been classified as neurotic for being excessive, protracted, associated with irrational despair and hopelessness, and preoccupied with the fear of personal death. These classifications lack solid supporting evidence, however.

Depression is the most frequently observed excessive symptom (Osterweis et al., 1984). Unfortunately it is difficult to differentiate between the depressed feelings or sadness of bereavement, labeled by some as reactive depression, and clinical depression; several symptoms such as anorexia, weight loss, and sleep disturbance are common to both. (See Table 5.1.)

There are interesting relationships between the nature and extent of morbidity associated with bereavement and the deterioration of physical health. Considerable evidence exists of a link between disease in specific organ systems and bereavement, for example, the cardiovascular system. Sudden cardiac arrhythmias, myocardial infarction, and congestive heart failure are the most frequently mentioned conditions. But other than for these impairments, studies generally do not find increases in physician visits or hospitalization following bereavement in the United States, unlike those in Great Britain (Osterweis et al., 1984). Nevertheless there are reported increases in drinking, smoking, and reliance upon drugs, especially tranquilizers, habits that could indicate a general disregard for the maintenance of sound health.

Who would deny the seriousness of any client's expressed thoughts of suicide? This is especially true for the bereaved. Osterweis and associates (1984) report that national statistics for the United States from 1949 to 1951 established that suicide rates were higher among the widowed than among their married counterparts, especially among elderly men, data that since have been confirmed by numerous reliable studies. In perspective, however, it must be remembered that many of the bereaved report thinking about death often and in many different ways. These thoughts may not necessarily be damaging; they could be essential aspects of the religious and spiritual reconstruction in which many of the bereaved engage.

What can be said in summary about difficult grieving? Perhaps the best statement is Raphael's (1983) conclusion that those least able to cope with grief are "those with the fewest personal or social resources, those who are already physically or emotionally unwell, those already under stress or

who have already demonstrated a poor resolution of past losses, or those
who hold themselves personally accountable in some way for the death"
(p.336).

SUMMARY

After completing even this truncated review, it is easier to understand
how bereavement most often is viewed as a psychic response. But that is
a limited and limiting perspective. It is time now to examine what has so
far been omitted—the religious and spiritual issues associated with bereavement. I shall do that by examining, in chapter 3, how some psychologists and psychoanalysts have attempted to reconcile their concepts with
religious and spiritual thinking.

Chapter 3

The Psyche and the Spirit

To the practitioner the most commanding and immediate effects of grief are the emotional reactions. It is no wonder that these responses have commanded the most attention of scientists as well. The reasons are understandable: A person's pain must be lessened, the preoccupation with the deceased reduced, and the thoughts focused so that some order can be brought to daily living. The griever must bridge the isolation that has cut off badly needed warmth and support from friends and family. Guilt and blame that has battered the self-image must be overcome.

Eventually, of course, for most people, the obvious, overt signs of grief disappear. We have been taught by conventional wisdom and much of the literature that this signals the end of bereavement. But some authorities are aware that other, more covert disruptions that occur to the personality may linger even after the bereaved appear to be functioning well day by day.

Simos (1979), Parkes and Weiss (1983), and Shuchter (1986), for example, explain this less obvious time of bereavement as the continued search by the griever for a different identity. Schuchter reports this comment by one of the widows he studied:

> I really don't feel there was much left of me. I really didn't know what I was or who I was or what kind of being I was. It seemed it always revolved about the two of us all the time. Your total self, how you cope—it seems like it always just revolves around two people. Even just thinking about something, I would say to myself, "Well, I know that David would think the other way." He was such a part of everything I did that it was a total aloneness . . . I'm beginning to find myself now, and I'm beginning to feel good about this, because what I'm finding out is really neat (p. 266).

The need for a new identity is particularly important for someone whose life has been closely bonded to the deceased, but it can occur as a conse-

37

quence of any meaningful loss of a person, ideal, symbol, or organizational affiliation that leaves the griever's world, and his or her place in it, much different.

Many people are not up to these personal challenges; life is more than they can handle well. But many others rise to the occasion. Glick and coauthors (1974) find that many subjects in the Harvard Study felt they had become stronger and more confident people. Similar results are reported from San Diego—by the end of 2 years the majority of widows and widowers were able to regard their grief as "growth promoting" (Shuchter, 1986). They saw themselves as more realistic, spiritual, patient, sensitive, autonomous, assertive, and open. Their experiences enabled them to put things in perspective and to appreciate more important things in life. Kessler (1987), too, demonstrates that many of her subjects regarded bereavement as liberating: over half mentioned feeling freed from previously limiting ties.

CHANGES IN WORLD VIEW

Most of those findings are characterized by researchers as changes in self-image, but they can be interpreted also as indications of even more fundamental changes. Shuchter (1986) describes these as alterations of people's "world views." A world view, he explains, is the set of beliefs people have about how the universe functions and what place they, as individuals, occupy therein. Some may refer to these beliefs, as did Jung (1957), as a person's philosophy of life; Pelletier (1978) and Ferguson (1980) are two who use the concept of "personal paradigm," borrowing from the work of Thomas Kuhn (1962). There are many ways of describing how humans organize and give consistency to their lives and the world, but we shall use the construct of world view in this section.

Few people ever bother to articulate their world view; words fail them and images are so indistinct that they find themselves limited to a few inexact and inadequate clichés ("the early bird gets the worm," or "God helps those who help themselves"). Bellah et al. (1985) observe that few people can "express the fullness of being that is actually theirs" (p. 81). Yet we all possess a set of generalized beliefs about whether things are going well or not, whether people are to be trusted or guarded against. We all need to assume something about how people function toward one another, in love and anger, as friends or competitors. The same applies toward organizations and institutions, such as the government, churches, and unions. From these interactions we devise a sense about and image of such abstractions as truth, justice, and security (Raphael, 1983). We then personalize these generalizations, turning them from views of the universe to views of my universe (Carse, 1981). Kelly (1963) points out that we need these assumptions to gain confidence that the way we respond to a given situation will, in turn, produce an understandable response from others.

A world view is more than cognitive images, however. Carse (1981) writes about a web of perceptions, feelings, images, and values that each person spins from specific personal experiences. This web is best revealed through the decisions we make and act upon in specific situations (Smith, 1982). Hence our world view is constantly being extended and altered to account for and accommodate new perceptions and knowledge. We view daily experiences through this web and react to events and ideas accordingly.

Everyday, minor changes in world view are usually handled easily. But when a major event occurs, such as the death of a loved one, the web itself can become unstable (Schneider, 1984). Many aspects of one's personalized world then become suspect and open to question and revision. Parkes and Weiss (1983) describe how some of their bereaved subjects gradually abandoned one set of views and substituted new ones. A case from my own clinical work illustrates this process. A widower in his early forties said:

> Life used to be so dependable. I worked and brought in the money and A. took care of the house and did the shopping, looked after the kids and bought their clothes. That's how my parents did it and my grandparents, too, I guess. Now, I don't know; I've got to be mother and father. I'd like to remarry soon, but it won't be the same, especially for the kids. They're going to need more from me than before. Can I do that and continue my career, too? That's really what I do best, you know; what I've enjoyed most. Sometimes I wonder if it will stay that way.

This man was adjusting to new realities. His career had been successful in part because of the time and the priority he had given to it. His priorities had worked well for him because his wife had been a willing participant in this system. Her untimely death forced him to consider other arrangements, attitudes, and values. Marital roles for both partners the next time around would have to be redefined, concepts of family management reexamined. Underneath these concerns, however, was a new awareness of the impermanence of marriage—and of all meaningful relationships. If his 39-year-old wife could die, how much time did he have in life?

Losing confidence in vital aspects of one's fundamental values, beliefs, and understandings is threatening and anxiety provoking. Shuchter (1986) writes,

> The tragedy challenges one's beliefs in the goodness of God, the predictability and control of life and one's self, the limitlessness of life, the value of one's efforts or of 'saving for a rainy day,' or the optimism one has felt throughout life. When such beliefs are at first challenged, there is usually nothing to replace them immediately, and the bereaved experience a void,

an absence of belief. They have no sense of direction or of a future purpose—especially since their purpose in life and their plans for the future had
relied heavily on a relationship that no longer exists (pp. 283–284).

The bereaved, their beliefs shaken, often enter an uncertain time, and
operate on a day-to-day basis without being quite sure why they are doing
things. They have learned that people cannot have complete personal
control over themselves and the environment. A major personal crisis can
result, especially if at first there appears to be no acceptable set of substitute beliefs and aspirations. Carse (1981) refers to this as the "cosmic
nature of grief" (p. 5), when the universe no longer makes any sense.
Decisions become more difficult to make and the results more questionable. The man cited above found himself vacillating for many months
between job priorities and home obligations, first favoring one, then the
other. For many months he remained in what Shuchter (1986) calls a
holding pattern that allowed him to function day-by-day, but left him
unable to make major decisions. Putting one's shattered world view back
together takes time—for some a lifetime.

Is a disorganized world view another way of identifying difficult grieving? Possibly. Is the process of reconstruction of clinical interest? Yes, both
because the person's world view is askew and because of the continuing
difficulties he or she is likely to encounter as a consequence. It is this
process of building anew, the questioning and searching for new answers,
that must be closely observed and possibly guided.

As indicated earlier, a notable shift in world outlook can occur as a
consequence of any significant life event—a birth, divorce, marriage, rite
of passage, or catastrophic loss. But many believe that reactions to a death
are the most upsetting. As Becker (1973) maintains, "the idea of death, the
fear of it, haunts the human animal like nothing else; it is a mainspring of
human activity . . ." (p. ix). The death of someone significant brings the
survivor face to face with his or her personal mortality.

From childhood on we all incorporate into our psychological structures
a knowledge of death's inevitability. Usually this is accommodated by
establishing defenses as protection against the harsh reality of nonbeing.
Children may at first believe themselves to be immortal. When evidence
accumulates that no living thing is exempt from death, other defenses are
established, such as that death occurs only to the very old. At some point
each adult realizes that he has lived out a great deal of his life; Jaques (1973)
sees that this is one of the principal causes of the mid-life crisis. Levinson
and associates (1978, p. 51) find that "some preoccupation with death—
fearing it, being drawn to it, seeking to transcend it" is prevalent in what
they call "times of transition" from one life stage to another.

Each person's world view, once rendered vulnerable, probably must have to be reconstructed before he can again become fully engaged in life. Kessler (1987) is one of the many who sees that people can grow from adversity if they are willing to let themselves fully experience some of the frightening consequences such as aloneness, their own mortality, and greater freedom and self-responsibility. Such growth does not come easily. Carse (1981) remarks that people's discovery during grief that they are free to rebuild their lives along ways similar to or more satisfactory than before is frightening. This probably explains the comment of a widow who confided to me how at times she preferred not to be learning so much about herself in bereavement because she was beginning to feel obligated to help others. "That's scary," she admitted. Frankl (1978) might judge her remark to be an example of people's ability to rise above themselves, thereby finding greater meaning to existence.

The belief in adversity as an opportunity for personal growth is espoused by many clinicians, only a few of whom need be cited here. Switzer (1970) sees that grief can promote greater self-responsibility, which in turn promotes greater personal authenticity. Pollock (1987) goes further and views the mourning-liberation process as being similar to psychoanalytic "working through" of conflicts, defenses, and the lifting of repression. Kessler (1987) studied 31 men and women who reported much positive growth and maturity from bereavement, such as: a sharpening interest in life itself; a focusing on the future with openness and renewed hope; an increased confidence in their ability to deal with freedom; an increased sense of liberation; a deeper meaning of God and faith. Peck (1978) sees changes like these as essential in bringing the conscious self-concept into progressively greater congruence with reality. He calls this part of one's spiritual growth.

PSYCHOLOGY AND SPIRITUALITY

The term spirituality does not often appear in mainline psychological and psychoanalytical thinking, especially in the research literature. Fromm (1950) and Frankl (1975) maintain this is because academic psychology has been tied too closely to the natural sciences and laboratory methods of weighing, counting, and objective reporting. It has failed, thereby, to deal with vital human phenomena such as love, reason, conscience, values, and spirituality. Peck (1978), too, sees scientists in general as suffering from "tunnel vision" and hampered by concerns for methodology. Psychoanalysts, Frankl (1978) adds, have been particularly skeptical of all kinds of religious or philosophical statements and have been prone to view them as obsessional thinking that need not be taken seriously. He sees this attitude as overlooking matters of "the soul," which is one way of thinking about humankind's higher powers of consciousness. While he acknowledges that psychoanalysts cannot be expected to be theologians or philosophers, he nevertheless calls upon them to be concerned with the soul and its cure.

Kessler (1987) concludes that most of the psychiatric literature that attempts to explain human responses to loss relies too heavily upon biological, psychosocial, and psychodynamic constructs such as anxiety, depression, insecurity, and loss of control. She agrees with those who see such psychological concepts as symbols for deeper reactions. Some behavioral scientists and clinicians, however, have dared to bridge the gap between the fields of psychology and psychoanalysis on the one hand, and spirituality and religion on the other. It is to some of them that we now turn.

Jung (1957) provides a helpful starting place. He views the spirit as the life of the body seen from within. He confesses that it is a perplexing and ambiguous term that can connote courage and liveliness, refer to a ghost, or be used to characterize the degree of a social group's zest. The spirit to Jung is the quintessence of the life of the mind, just as "living being" is the quintessence of life of the body. In fact, he frequently uses "spirit" interchangeably with the concept of "mind." He writes: "spirit, like God, denotes an object of psychic experience which cannot be proved to exist in the external world and cannot be understood rationally" (p. 328). He also says, "once we have freed ourselves from the prejudices that we have to refer a concept either to objects of external experience or to a priori categories or reason, we can turn our attention and curiosity wholly to that strange and still unknown thing we call 'spirit.' " Frankl (1978) addresses spiritual issues under the label of "meta meaning," which he does not necessarily see as theistic. His God is a partner of intimate soliloquies reached by talking to oneself in utmost sincerity and solitude.

Fromm (1950) has not been concerned so much with whether a man embraces beliefs in God and formal religions but whether he pursues love and truth in life. He sees a subtle relationship between the connecting of "one with the All" and the process of breaking through the confines of one's organized self—the ego—to get in touch with the excluded and disassociated part of oneself, the unconscious. He calls upon therapy to aim beyond the goal of adjustment by helping clients to discover their optimal development, which he calls the "health of the soul." To him matters of the soul should not continue to be the exclusive purview of organized religions. The end result of religious experiences should be an awakened sense of wondering and questioning, the responsibility for which ultimately rests with the individual, not on the therapist or the clergy.

Hillman (1975) also uses religious terms. The soul to him is a reflective perspective on life. It deepens the meaning of events, expands imagination, and enhances love, made possible through its "special relation to death." The soul expresses itself differently than the psyche, by fantasies and dreams which, through the flow of impressions, give metaphorical sense to life. It is not a part of objective facts that require explanation but rather a part of subjective experiences that require understanding. The soul's disorders result in snarled communication, as a disrupted social nexus, or as frustrated spiritual fulfillment. None of these difficulties can be understood by using the medical model that predominates in psychology and psychoanalysis.

Some kind of construct of the unconscious appears to be vital to an understanding of human spirituality. Frankl (1975) divides the unconscious into two states, the instinctual and the spiritual. The instinctual state refers to the drives and to all our inherited and collective tendencies. The spiritual includes many phenomona like love, ethics, aesthetics, as well as the expression of spirituality itself. Others speak of a higher consciousness, a form of the unconscious, to explain spirit. Jung (1960) sees it to be superior to the ego-consciousness. Peck (1978) uses another term, transcendence. To him this means transforming one's nature. Frankl (1978) equates transcendence with relating, and being directed to something other than oneself, reaching out not only for a meaning to fulfill but also for humans to love. Das (1971) sees transcendence as a growth in personal autonomy and differentiated integration. Maslow (1971) differentiates between the transcendent and nontranscendent among self-actualizing people, although he confesses to finding some degree of transcendence among people who were not self-actualizers.

Transcenders have the following characteristics, according to Maslow (1971):

1. their peak experiences are common but important to them;
2. sacredness is perceived in all things;
3. values like beauty, goodness, unity, and transcendence itself are their most important motivations in life;
4. unity is sensed in the universe and within themselves; this leads to a cosmic consciousness;
5. they possess a profoundly religious or spiritual sense (not by ordinary definitions) that leads to an extraordinary humanness.

Reaching a transcendent state is a profoundly emotional, spiritual, even a mystical experience, but not necessarily in the form typically thought of as a religious conversion. Fromm (1950) asserts that similar feelings can result from successful therapy.

PSYCHOLOGY AND STATES OF HIGHER CONSCIOUSNESS

States of higher consciousness, separate from their relationship to religiousness, have been of interest to psychologists for many years. They are referred to as "altered forms of consciousness" or "altered states of consciousness" (ASC).

To Pelletier and Garfield (1976) an altered state of consciousness is one in which there has been a qualitative shift in mental functioning. An ASC differs from a normal state in that ordinary stimuli are processed in significantly different ways, usually viewed as atypical in Western culture. These experiences can increase emotional intensity, change body chemistry and neurophysiological responses, alter body image, produce disorders and delusions, and develop profound feelings and insights that lead to a sense of having discovered great truths. These are conditions reported by persons having profound religious experiences but are also similar to reactions by some people during the most acute stages of grief (Rees, 1971).

PSYCHOLOGY AND RELIGION

What have psychologists to say about religiosity separate from spirituality? Freud (1961) set the tone when he wrote, "religion would thus be the universal compulsive neurosis of mankind; like that of the child, it derives from the Oedipal complex, from the relationship to the father" (p. 43). That view was softened in later writings (Freud, 1964) but he seems to be best remembered for views that religion is of little concern to psychoanalysis beyond (a) speculation about why people formulate the idea of a god; and (b) considerations of the psychological needs that religion fulfills.

Freud's views helped to establish an early wedge between psychoanalysis and religion that prevails to this day. As Frankl (1975) observes, many psychoanalysts define religion merely in terms of sublimation, reducing all religious experiences, conscious or unconscious, to infantile sex origins. Bergin (1983) calls for constraint of this practice of attributing pathodynamic origins to values one disagrees with. Practitioners themselves, he reminds us, have spiritual tendencies even though they may be symbolized and expressed under many aliases; he cites survey evidence that leads him to conclude practicing psychologists are not, as most believe, that much less religious than the general public.

How have some of the other authorities in psychology and psychoanalytical thought viewed religion? Fromm (1950) defines religion as "any system of thought and action shared by a group which gives the individual a frame of orientation and an object of devotion" (p. 21). As a system religion counteracts people's disharmony within themselves and with nature. It is man's way of seeking equilibrium, to be achieved through devotion to an aim, an idea, or a power transcending humankind. Fromm (1950) believes religion and psychoanalysis complement each other in four ways: (a) through an increased human awareness that leads to greater religious feeling and devotion; (b) by reaffirmation of the importance of what is still unknown; (c) by an increased understanding of the use and value of rituals; and (d) by an increased understanding of the semantic aspect of religions, the symbol system being a vital clue to underlying human reality. Frankl (1975), too, sees religiousness as vital for human functioning. He defines it as a relationship between the innermost self and a transcendent diety or "Thou." A person's genuine religiousness, his personal relationship to God, must unfold spontaneously, in its own time. Both Fromm and Frankl claim that psychoanalysis has a religious function. Fromm defines this as fostering in clients independence, freedom, the recognition of truth, loving relationships, and the ability to listen to and follow one's conscience. Frankl believes that the psychiatrist must have a belief in God or in an ontological transcendent state in order to foster similar beliefs in the client.

Switzer (1970) acknowledges the importance of faith in bereavement. He does not use this term in its most popular sense, as belief without evidence, but endorses Tillich's (1957) definition of faith as an act of the whole being, the central force that is commitment to persons, causes, and what is meaningful in life. It is this return to commitment and engagement, Switzer sees, that is the necessary element in healing grief.

Hillman (1975) calls for a "revisioning" of psychology to recognize that it "does not take place without religion" (p. 228). He sees religion as helping psychology to better understand the depths of its activities and to acknowledge the fact that it, too, really can be a "practice" of religion. In short, each has much to teach the other.

Psychologists studying bereavement find it difficult at times to differentiate religious from psychological responses of people. Glick and associates (1974), for example, uncovered a significant minority of the widows studied who claimed that their faith had been shaken. Some needed an explanation for their husband's death beyond that provided by the medical report. Neither were they satisfied with simple religious homilies. Even the more religious widows, those who had no difficulty accepting death as the will of God, still found themselves searching for further explanations. Other widows, some of whom denied having had any kind of a spiritual experience, when questioned at greater length, admitted: (a) to believing that their lives had been shaped by powerful forces beyond their capacity to comprehend; and (b) to pondering recently about the meaning of God and immortality. Both of these responses have religious meanings.

Hospice workers do not find these results out of the ordinary. Many patients and family members who steadfastly maintain little or no interest in religion will express religious and spiritual concerns through "why" questions: Why me? Why now? Why not someone else? They will ponder whether some wrong they have committed might have caused the fatal condition. Patients, when reviewing their lives, will search for and reaffirm what has provided the most meaning and what they may have done to make a difference to those they love. Many hospice staff and volunteers have learned to be sensitive to clues that reflect religious and spiritual issues even when religious terms are absent, and they have learned not to turn them into psychological issues. To better understand that statement it is necessary to move on to the next chapter.

SUMMARY

This chapter, although brief, illustrates how intertwined the psyche and spirit are to some psychologists and psychiatrists. We have briefly reviewed how they have tried to explain human functioning by using concepts both from their own disciplines and from religion, theology, and philosophy. And we have attempted to relate some of their thinking to explanations about grief and bereavement.

It is time now to turn to theologians and philosophers for other concepts that help to explain human reactions to loss. This will provide a more expanded conceptual base for understanding the complexities of grief and bereavement.

Chapter 4

Bereavement as Spiritual Development and a Crisis in Faith

To set the stage for this chapter it is necessary to reiterate why the author sees matters of the spirit and faith to be so important in understanding bereavement. As stated in the opening chapter, the psychic and spiritual responses of humans to loss are intertwined. After a major loss the survivor's life may appear to have lost all meaning. It is not enough, therefore, that the counselor help to bring the bereaved through the emotional crisis alone; that would be like a physician discharging a patient after merely toning down a fever and leaving an infection or disease untreated. A person in grief may need help reviewing, perhaps reconstructing, his sense of purpose and identity in life, that is, spiritual and religious issues.

Most psychological practitioners could justifiably protest that they are not prepared to work with religious matters. Robb (1986) maintains that psychologists have received "virtually no formal training" to work with "broad issues" (p. 88). The obvious solution, to refer clients to a religious counselor, is not always the most beneficial option, in part because of lack of preparation by pastoral counselors on matters of bereavement (Doka & Jendreski, 1986), and because this bifurcation of services implies an unnatural separation of the spiritual and religious from the psychological and sociological.

One of the basic principles of this book is that psychological practitioners who wish to help the bereaved not only can, but must, prepare themselves to actively assist their clients to reconstruct a new sense of meaning and purpose—to redefine what they most respect in life (what is holy and divine), and to realize what they will commit themselves. This life-long task, while formidable, is not as difficult to undertake as most novices (or those who see themselves as novices) believe—because most of us probably know more about religious and spiritual matters than we are immediately aware of. Almost every person, and especially psychological practitioners who are predisposed toward self-reflection, has religious and spiritual awareness, whether or not they are devoted to and tutored in a specific religion.

This chapter has several purposes: (a) to help those who believe they are nonreligious or those for whom religious and spiritual matters occupy a marginal part of their lives to discover and claim their latent or fragmented religiousness and better integrate it into psychological constructs; and (b) to assist those who practice a specific religion to better understand how they might work with clients outside that faith. It is important, therefore, that we review constructs of spirituality, religion, and some related topics in more detail.

SPIRITUALITY DEFINED

Spirituality is not easy to "define"—an intellectual task—for the spirit can be realized only in part by the conscious mind. Spirituality affects all the senses and may be detected in the unconscious psyche as well. Translating its complexities into words, even for poets, is elusive.

It helps to think of the spirit in two ways. The first is the force that creates and propels life in all animals and plants. The spirit sends out new tendrils and leaves from a plant stalk, and drives the spermatozoa upward into the fallopian tube. It is what keeps a human clinging to life in impossible conditions such as those in Nazi concentration camps. Singh (1959) refers to it as the vital flame in man.

Spirituality also describes that which encourages or induces humans, and possibly other life forms, to seek out, nurture, and appreciate the good, the beautiful, and the truthful in life. It is the impulse toward wholeness and harmony, that which leads humankind to discover and create the new and the better; not only because it makes life easier and more understandable, but because the process of discovery and creativity brings joy and pleasure. The spirit fosters life's fullest flowering, the development of its greatest potential.

At workshops I frequently ask people to describe remembered spiritual experiences. Some find spiritual moments in everyday incidents—during violin practice, while jogging along solitary wooded paths, or when checking on sleeping children in a moonlit room. A man recalled a treasured moment when his 4-year-old looked up at him during a walk to say, "I love you."

Others recall more dramatic incidents. One man reminisced about a college spring break when he and his best friend, facing the ocean at sunset, talked deeply about their lives and friendship; "it became as if we were floating in space," he concluded. A woman remembered two distinctly different kinds of experiences, both of which produced powerful reactions: as a youth seeing Mt. Rainier for the first time; and many years later, as a volunteer in a local prison, being told by a young convict, "I wish you were my Mom." Another woman told of the time when, alone with a supposedly comatose grandmother, she nevertheless reminisced aloud about happy moments together, and the old woman suddenly sat up, said, "Lynn, you're so pretty," and died.

These are spiritual experiences that can occur to almost everyone. We are buoyed by moments of fulfillment and mystery; during a romance, a birth, or a successful venture. They become moments of wonder, joy, and thankfulness that can take the breath away and temporarily cause the world to look different. They are moments of high energy and enthusiasm expressed by exclamations, a leap into the air, or tears of joy. There is an instantaneous connecting with others, an outburst of love and caring, a oneness with the world.

The spirit produces far greater effects than these few idyllic moments, however, if given the opportunity. Foster (1978, p. 2) believes that it can liberate people from "the stifling slavery to self-interest and fear," setting them free to live a full life. Fox (1972), too, finds that discovering the spiritual world allows humans to transcend concerns for security, status, and ego trips. Spirituality brings humans more into contact and confrontation with reality (Ochs, 1983); for Fox this means honesty with the self.

Some readers at this point may find these views differing from more widely-accepted definitions. We in the Western civilization tend to view the spiritual life as the purview of holy people who have withdrawn from temporal living to devote themselves to prayer and meditation. The authorities quoted in this chapter see spiritual growth as possible for all people, including those with unglamorous and tedious jobs (Foster, 1978; Fox, 1972). Another author who agrees is Sinetar (1986), in a book entitled *Ordinary People as Monks and Mystics.* For Ochs (1983), too, spirituality must enhance the everyday and commonplace.

The spirit waxes and wanes within us. Even though the urge to live fully, and not just exist, is present from an individual's first breath and bouyed by fulfilling times, love affairs, births, and accomplishments, it also is drained by tragedies, mistakes, disappointments, divorces, loss of myths or dreams, and, especially, deaths. Death defies and contradicts the spirit; it is easy for the bereaved to conclude that their lassitude is justifiable, for death appears to be the ultimate fulfillment to which they should be dedicated, not life. The spirit in abeyance leaves the bereaved chronically tired, drains away their vitality, and decimates their hope and desire. If allowed to persist too long, Harper (1968) warns, the spirit can be suffocated and replaced by boredom. The critical task of the bereaved is to rejuvenate the spirit.

Our inherent spirituality does not fully flower, however, without conscious attention. Daily living can dull our sensitivity to the spirit, allowing it to flag. To counteract those tendencies, our spirituality must be tended to, just as the physical body must be kept in shape. Foster (1986) calls for the disciplines of spiritual life that involve daily attention to rituals usually, but not necessarily, practiced within a spiritual community. Times of quiet retreats, when the body and mind are rested and there are opportunities for unhurried self-reflection, are necessary.

Even when it is not possible to get away, there are other ways of renewing the spirit. Prayer, for Fox (1972), is a vital sustainer of spirituality, but he does not necessarily refer to the kind of ritualistic prayers associated with most formal religions. Any form of meditation that enhances awareness of life is prayer. It is a recollection of life and its mysteries. A prayerful disposition, he says, is the willingness to raise vital questions about life. The spirit is renewed by expressing basic beliefs through action.

With attention, the spirit can develop from occasional moments of exaltation into more extreme or higher states of mystical consciousness. Sinetar (1986) describes several stages in becoming truly mystical.

1. The beginning, intuitional state is an inner prompting, usually expressed in sudden moments of insight that reveal there is more to life than ordinary living.
2. The next state is expressed by pulling away, as a response to the need to distance oneself from a given way of life that has been shaped by programmed goals, cultural beliefs, and family expectations—most of which were shaped at childhood.
3. The following state is characterized by a strengthened awareness of truths or personal reality.
4. Finally there develops a commitment to devote one's life to a complete and intimate relationship with one's deity, dwelling in a world unknown to other humans. This entails a radical restructuring of the self that is expressed by different behavior toward others, and a shift in interest away from social and material concerns toward the supernatural world.

Along the way there develops a higher or cosmic consciousness. Some refer to this state as an understanding of and union with God or the divine plan. It may appear as a temporary state but with attention can become an ongoing process lasting from several months to many years. During that time a person might pass in and out of different states of consciousness, but the overall condition is a much more complex state of awareness and wisdom.

This higher consciousness should not be mistaken for spiritualism or belief in the existence of spirits apart from matter or a belief in the survival of the human personality. Neither should it be confused with communication between the living and the dead, mesmerism, trance-like states, or the gift of tongues. These may or may not play a role in the development of greater spirituality but are not essential to the central themes of this chapter.

The hard work and sacrifices necessary for growth to higher stages is well-rewarded: Singh (1959) writes about greater self-realization and God-realization or, as Fox (1972) expresses it, a full, rich life. Ochs (1983) refers to growth that leads to transformation and enlargement of our being and consciousness, a recentering of the self that fosters greater nurturing, and more meaningful relationships. These are different goals, she notes, than the traditional, male-oriented writings usually address.

These references to higher states of consciousness are included in this section not to suggest that bereavement counselors need to become spiritual mystics, but to introduce the developmental nature of spiritual growth. If everyone has a spiritual nature and this nature can develop from an elementary to a more complex form both in response to conscious and unconscious experiences then it follows that in any human relationship there will be differences in spiritual levels. It is not a matter, as many people suppose, of one person who is devoid of spirituality confronting a second who is spiritual. There will always be common ground for the two to join in mutual awareness. It is a matter of finding the language that will help in making those connections.

One example might suffice. Frequently the bereaved pull back from social contacts, spending much time alone. Spiritually this can be explained as the need for solitude, which allows the person to reshape beliefs and images of the world in which he or she lives. Far too often the need for solitude is viewed as something temporary that will and should pass, and not as an opportunity to strengthen and develop spiritual tendencies.

It should also be obvious by this time that there are ways of examining and explaining spirituality without resorting to formal religious terminology. Spirituality need not have anything to do with institutionalized religions (Singh, 1959). The same can be said about religiosity. Let us examine how religiousness differs from spirituality on the one hand and formal religious behavior on the other.

RELIGIOSITY

Religiosity is developmental. To understand that statement we must first find a way of understanding religiousness that will provide a common understanding among people of different church affiliations, or between those with formal religious training and those with little or none.

It is important at the onset to note James' (1960) warning about oversimplified definitions; he suspected that there was neither one specific and essential kind of religious object, nor one specific and essential kind of religious act. This may account for Corless' (1986) conclusion that while there are many definitions of religiosity, "perspicuity" is rare. She cites the comments of Ulanov: to be religious is to be conscious of the connection to an extra-mundane authority that is beyond oneself, beyond one's parents, beyond one's society. The key term, she maintains, is "extra-mundane authority." Agreeing again with Ulanov, she sees religiousness as an openness to experience.

The religious person is one who achieves direct knowledge of ultimate reality to which he or she becomes devoted (Glock, 1962). MacLean (1988) adds that religion provides meaning to living in ways that connect one to the sense of the ultimate in life, sometimes described as the cosmos. After participating in an exercise frequently used by death awareness workshops designed merely to relax participants, one women reported that by following the verbal instructions to imagine floating in space, she was suddenly aware of and felt connected to everyone she knew, even those who had died, in some unexplainable way. What she experienced could have been that religious sense of oneness with the vastness of all forms of life.

Religiosity is more complex than that, however. Glock (1962) describes five ways religiosity is manifested:

1. the experiential—defined as subjective—emotional responses;
2. the ritualistic—the expected performance of specified practices;
3. the ideological, expressed as specified beliefs;
4. the intellectual—those basic tenets of faith; and
5. the consequential—those secular expressions of all of the above, a person's good works.

It is difficult for people all by themselves to find ways of expressing their religious interests and urges, which explains, in part, why formal religions attract adherents. Religious faiths and bodies inspire religious development and channel religious expression—which become the differences that separate people. Often these differences appear to be greater than they are because it is assumed that each person fully believes every tenet of their adopted belief. This is seldom the case.

Proudfoot (1985) explains that regardless of the religious tradition a person practices, the religious experience has to be individually expressed. This means it will differ in certain ways, both in thinking and practice, from the formal creeds the membership professes in public religious ceremonies. There is hardly uniformity of beliefs and practices, even within the most militant religious groups. This fact allows almost any two people, if they search diligently, to find common experiences and beliefs.

This individual interpretation of religion is markedly different than what many established churches teach. But Singh (1959) sees that God made man and man made religions. All the religions of the world, including Hinduism, Buddhism, Christianity, came into existence to serve primary human needs according to the exigencies of then-prevailing conditions.

Campbell (1988), too, believes there is an individual basis to religiousness. For him religion in all cultures grows out of mythology. Myth is metaphor, he says, a life-shaping image that rests deep within each of us, what he calls our life system. The imagery of mythology incorporates spiritual symbols. The meaning of the Holy Grail, for example, is the adult's search for the dynamic source in his life, that which was present in childhood but lost in adulthood. These and many other myths are shared across cultures and are capable of arousing great feelings. Religions help to shape and dignify those myths and feelings, but they also misinterpret myths, he maintains, by attributing historical referents to symbols, which more properly should be spiritual metaphors.

Religions serve many other valuable purposes, one of which is to provide hopeful explanations for what happens after death. People need relief from the terrible fear of the complete end to everything in their lives, and the total separation from all that is important (Freese, 1977). It is this concept of an afterlife that explains much of the attractiveness of religious thought throughout humankind's existence on this planet, he maintains. It also provides another plot of common ground among all people: the need to work out for themselves some explanation of death that will alleviate the fears of that unknown state.

What of mystical religious experiences? They can be thought of in two ways: as higher developmental states; and as altered mental and/or physiological states, the most serious of which are psychotic breaks. Not everyone is capable of having mystical experiences. Those who do can be thought of as possessing a rare talent. To ignore the content and importance of their mystical moments by writing them off as hallucinations or childish fantasies is to overlook possibly significant aspects of religious expression. On the other hand, counselors must be alert to when religiousness is the expression of an abnormality, when it is used to suppress pathology, or when it operates as a stressor to exacerbate existing weaknesses and problems (Spilka, 1986).

THE DEVELOPMENTAL NATURE
OF FAITH

The mystical nature of religion may obscure rather than further explain how religiosity develops within individuals. A more profitable approach may be through an understanding of faith.

What is Personal Religious Faith?

Before turning to the thinking of learned scholars, it is interesting to review how the laity describe faith. In a telephone interview survey conducted by the Religious Education Association, *Faith Development in the Adult Life Cycle* (FD/ALC) (Stokes, 1987), more than 1,000 people in the United States were asked this question. The majority saw faith in terms of a relationship, most frequently with God, but also with people, causes, or ideas. Smaller percentages reported faith as finding meaning in life or a set of beliefs. A low percentage (4%) viewed faith as membership in a church or synagogue. To researchers these data suggest that beneath the creeds people's faith is based on personal relationships rather than formal affiliations.

Fowler (1981), who developed a six-stage theory of faith development from interviews of 359 persons, has also concluded that faith is relational: there is always someone or something to which the person expresses trust and loyalty. It is a way of seeing our everyday life in relation to images of "the ultimate conditions of our existence."

Fowler (1981), influenced by Tillich, sees faith as "the state of being ultimately concerned" (p. 4). As such it demands the total commitment of mind and personality that can result in gratifying fulfillment. The test for the ultimate (Tillich, 1957) is whether objects of faith remain absolute, infinite, and unconditional. The more one's faith deals with divine absolutes, however these are imaged, is the extent to which the person is enlarged. This provides a confidence, some say power, that sustains and undergirds one's life. Fowler explains this transcendence as the "X" factor that mysteriously enriches our lives.

One can have faith in many causes or movements or even in "economic success" and "political power." Many people make minor gods of human relationships, with a spouse, lover, or child; and also of institutions like the family, the church, or their employing institution. When any of these significant human relations are destroyed, by death or other causes, or the institutions appear to have violated the trust a person placed in them, the victim's faith is shaken. Consider King Lear who was committed to his family and the political and military systems of his kingdom. They all failed him. Life lost its meaning and its trustworthiness. He was unable before his death to recreate faith in a new, more reliable sense of the ultimate in which he could find stability.

People usually can identify most of their greatest loyalties—spouse, employing organization, labor union, church community, veterans' organization, for example. But it is not easy for them to detect their ultimate allegiances. One way is to ask what they would be willing to die for. If that is too extreme, then ask what they would be willing to suffer great humiliation to preserve. One client, who thought he was willing to sacrifice his marriage and family to foster a career, nevertheless discovered to his surprise, when questioned, that he would sacrifice his life only for his child. From this single question followed a reappraisal of some of the basic assumptions on which he had lived the past few years of his life.

Fowler (1981) lists several questions that individuals might ask of themselves to help determine their faith commitments:

- What commands and receives my best time and energy?
- What causes, dreams, goals, or institutions am I pouring out my life for?
- What power or powers do I fear or dread? What power or powers do I rely on and trust?
- To what or whom am I committed in life? In death?
- With whom or what group do I share my most sacred and private hopes for life and for the lives of those I love?
- What are those most sacred hopes, those most compelling goals and purposes of my life?

The "answers" each of us construct for the kinds of questions Fowler raises are not always put into verbal messages. Tillich (1957) describes faith as acts of commitment. These can be recognized in specific, concrete situations such as how we donate time and money: one person helps the less fortunate, another enhances the power and prestige of an organization. Yet beneath those public acts may lie deeper commitments that can be identified most of the time only through vague feelings and images; some people are able to express them artistically, musically, or metaphorically. Only in times of crisis, when the deepest structures of the self are disturbed, when the most basic fears are aroused—from an anonymous telephone death threat, the threatened loss of job position, or from the loss of a loved one, for example—can some of these basic commitments come into play.

Most people reshape faith commitments several times in a lifetime. As teenagers they might elevate a peer group or commitment to school activities above the loyalty they once gave to family, only to replace that in a few years with a commitment to marriage. Loyalty to country or a given unit in the army might become elevated above all other commitments for some young men. Fowler's in-depth interviews reported in *Stages of Faith* trace how some people's image of and relationship to God shift over time.

People do not always have a well-integrated, compatible set of faith commitments. There can be, and perhaps usually are, conflicting loyalties to family and compassion on the one hand, and to images of manhood, respectability, and community on the other. A person may be able to live with potentially conflicting assumptions and commitments for many years—until a situation forces a choice among loyalties. Such has occurred for some parents when their child returned home with AIDS.

Resolving these conflicts is usually trying, prompting stress and anxieties and testing people's tolerence for ambiguity and uncertainty. It is no wonder so many attempt to simplify their lives by living out fantasies of what their lives once were, becoming involved in the heaven-on-earth some religious sect is creating, or bringing about the righteous life through crusading for a single issue.

The problem with placing faith in simplistic ideologies, causes, religions, or relationships is that they can be incongruous with reality and fail along the way. The test for the ultimate commitment, Tillich (1957) stresses, is whether the objects of faith remain absolute, infinite, and unconditional; otherwise, when they fail, the person is left worse off than before. Life then becomes darker when there seems to be no person, ideal, symbol, or God to hold on to. The resulting solitude, Harper (1968) explains, leads to terrible suffering.

This is the kind of suffering and confusion faced by so many of the bereaved. It becomes intensified by the confrontation with the fact of death. The bereaved continually ask: Is this all life has to offer? What sense is there to go on living when we all die in the end? What kind of God would allow this to happen? Whatever "answers" are formulated or sensed involve the individual with the infinite, with faith.

It must be remembered that faith commitments and images tend to be shaped by and to support a person's entire system of values, opinions, and expectations. A man who falls in love, for example, expects to be loved in return and to have many values and opinions reaffirmed by the loved one. If this happens, his faith assumptions involving romantic love, trust, family, and community are strengthened. These and many other aspects of his life can form a dynamic, coordinated system that enables him to operate day by day with confidence and consistency. When any significant portion of this system fails, other vital parts of the entire system may become questionable. Such people must then devote considerable time and energy to reconciling the inconsistencies, to bringing everything back into compatibility and order, producing again a dynamic equilibrium.

Life is a constant cycle of the breaking and remaking of our faith assumptions and commitments. The naivité of youth must be replaced because of the exigencies of young adulthood, and more mature commitments will in turn be altered by circumstances of middle or later adulthood. It may appear for some who verbalize throughout life the religious catechisms or creeds learned as children that there has been little, if any, alteration. The changes are revealed only through probing interviews, such as those used by both Stokes (1987) and Fowler.

Fowler (1981) sees that what we commit ourselves to through faith shapes our identities. These commitments determine and are determined by the communities we join. Tillich (1957) agrees saying that only in community can a people develop the content of their ultimate concern and actualize their faith. But we must be careful, Fowler warns, for there is a tendency for people nowadays to commit themselves to many different centers of value and power, for example, political movements, environmental causes, and self-help groups, as well as religions. He refers to this as being polytheistic, a pattern of faith and identity that lacks any one center of value and power sufficient to transcend and order one's life. People can get caught up in what Becker (1973) calls *causa sui* projects that foster worship of the human ego.

Beliefs

It is important to differentiate between beliefs and faith. Beliefs occupy an important place in a person's religiousness; they are the attempt to give verbal expression to one's faith. The two might also be thought of as being arranged along a continuum, beliefs being less complex and more consciously understood and expressed. A person can believe, for example, that if he or she works diligently and honestly the employer will reward him or her. Such a belief may be based on a faith assumption that the world is basically rational, so even if the person is not rewarded for good service, he or she may still contend that there is a good explanation for the boss's behavior. Or, to use an example closer to the topic of this book, one can believe that good nutritional and health habits will extend life, or at least improve the quality of those years remaining. But if a friend who has followed those prescriptions is striken with cancer, other beliefs may have to be substituted, ones that will not necessarily alter the underlying faith assumptions. (Quite likely we all tend to take the course that will require the fewest changes in beliefs and faith.)

A Developmental Theory of Faith

Fowler (1981) sees that humans begin building their faith system in infancy from relationships with their parents and other caretakers; the early years through childhood may be the most critical. A child raised on the street, for example, can learn that life is filled with horrors and constant disappointments, society's institutions being the enemy. Only dishonesty seems to pay, and honor is achieved by outwitting the respectable. In contrast, a student in highly favored circumstances might conclude that she or he should be prepared to become part of a small, elite group of people who are destined to control the affairs of the nation. Each child as he or she grows into adolescence will make decisions consistent with those assumptions, the consequences of which usually reenforce prior beliefs.

Faith, like the body and personality, unfolds and changes throughout life. Fowler, currently the most renowned advocate and theorist of the developmental view, sees six stagelike, developmentally related styles of faith:

1. the undifferentiated faith of infancy;
2. intuitive-projected faith of childhood, adopted from family and trusted older persons, mythic and literal;
3. synthetic-conventional faith—an extension of the creeds of organized religions;
4. individuative-reflective faith—the process of seeking one's individual faith;
5. conjunctive faith—the results of stage 4, a uniquely individual faith;
6. universalizing faith—a state approaching sainthood.

These stages are interrelated, forming a rising spiral, each successive step linked and adding to the person's previous faith. Each stage marks the rise of new capacities and strengths. Certain life issues recur at each stage but always in more complex form. The movement is toward a widening of vision, a shift in values, and an increase in certainty of self and relationships with others, even though there will be periods of unsettling confusion.

Stages have some relationship to chronological age, the first being characteristic of young children, stages 3 and 4 typical of young adults. But movement along the staged path is highly individualized. Regression to aspects of an earlier stage, especially during times of crisis, is possible.

Most people (roughly two-thirds of the population to generalize from both the Fowler study and the FD/ALC study samples [Stokes, 1987]) fall into stages 3 and 4. Stage 3, synthetic-conventional faith, is essentially a tacit system of values, prescriptions, and images about which the person feels deeply but which remain largely unexamined; stage 3 people tend to be very literal about their faith, the symbols not being separated from what they symbolize. In stage 4—individuative-reflective faith—the individual takes greater responsibility for his or her own commitments, life-style, beliefs, and attitudes.

It is not clear from the Fowler or Stokes descriptions whether movement to a higher faith stage operates independently from, or mostly in concert with, other aspects of personal development. Both Fowler and Stokes see parallels in the theories of developmental and cognitive psychologists. Humans may question their faith assumptions during periods of transition just as they do their relationships, values, and other aspects of their lives. But many questions remain unanswered. Are the transitions to another level of faith part of the typical human process of maturation and development? Or can the questioning of faith occur independently of these crises, motivated mostly by human or divine inspiration? Do faith changes trigger other major developmental changes? And what part do religious conversions play in such questioning? (Fowler describes conversion as being a significant recentering of one's previous conscious or unconscious faith and spiritual images.) Clearly born-again religious people change many aspects of their lives.

These life transitions are difficult periods requiring many basic changes in the fabric of one's life (Levinson et al., 1978). Increased anxiety is one of the results (May, 1980). When human tragedies occur during a time of transition, anxieties probably are amplified. With the personality already stretched to cope with real and perceived changes, a loss through death further depletes energy reserves and overtakes already committed personal and interpersonal resources. This is especially true if the beliefs and faith assumptions held by the bereaved themselves are undergoing revision. This aspect of difficult grieving is not given the attention in the literature that it deserves.

The Fowler construct of developmental stages permits the psychological practitioners to gain perspective on the religious views of clients. Take as an example how a counselor might view a client who believes strongly that God punishes sinners. He caused his wife's death, he maintains, for having violated a pledge made many years before to serve God more attentively if his older child would not die from an accident. This can be a literal interpretation of the Old Testament dictum of "an eye for an eye." The husband accepts his punishment from God as just. He reveals aspects of Fowler's stage 3 and some regression to stage 2. But he need not remain there. He can be helped by gentle questioning to decide if this contractual relationship with a vindictive God is what he most desires. What might his wife desire for him if she were alive? Did he ever see God as more compassionate and forgiving? When? What was his life like then? When was he happier? Does God desire people to be happy? In time, with help, the client can begin to reflect stage 3 and stage 4 thinking—and to move on with his bereavement.

What part do human tragedies play in producing faith changes? Stokes (1989) sees a clear relationship between crises and faith development. He maintains that we are more likely to question our faith when our lives are in some degree of disequilibrium. Bereavement is one of those times when previously tacit values and assumptions that have guided our lives may be questioned. The person who provided a mirror for the griever's sense of self may be lost or rejected. Most important, many of the beliefs about God, goodness, and the relationships of people to one another may no longer make much sense. These are all signals that the person may be ready for movement, possibly in regression, but with help to a higher developmental stage. The psychological practitioner has an obligation to provide whatever assistance may be beneficial.

IMPACT OF TRAGEDY

There is one additional point of view from the religious literature that can have considerable value in working with the bereaved—the impact both on the client and the practitioner of the sense of tragedy encountered by the client. The mark of a tragedy is its reversal of everything one ordinarily takes for granted (Harper, 1968). After tragedy life cannot be depended on in the same way it was previously. People may lose something that gave meaning to their lives; or which, at least, seemed to be one of the preconditions of a life—spouse, family, or health. When this happens, they often ask if there is any sense to living, especially if the death was senseless and with no redeeming value. A mother of two small children dies during her third childbirth due to a physician's carelessness. A young child is killed by a drunk driver. In each case the survivors can have some of their faith assumptions and religious views shattered; this leaves them confounded, perhaps paralyzed for a time.

Tragedy confronts both the client and practitioner with suffering and pain. McGill (1982) reminds us that the Western world is particularly uncomfortable with the concept of pain. Those who bring it up in conversations are suspect. Ours is a society that is engaged in the pursuit of happiness. Technology has given us control over physical pain and much environmentally caused suffering. The result has been the expectation of a pain-free society. When pain appears, something must have gone wrong. The doctor must have erred or the hospital must not have provided adequate service. When we become ill we often tend to blame ourselves, for allowing too much stress in our lives, or for failing to eat properly or exercise often enough.

If pain cannot be controlled, it is best denied. This postpones the suffering and the need to seek the cause. Advanced societies forget that pain and suffering, like death itself, is a natural part of living. To live well means not just to tolerate pain, but to learn the lessons it has to teach and, eventually, to transcend suffering. Pain provides the opportunity to gain a different balance and perspective in life. Harper (1968) comments that by not facing reality, one not only refuses to accept the inevitable, but also loses the chance to be exalted by the tragedy. Suffering allows humans to experience feelings, perceptions, and other aspects of themselves and life in general that can be known in no other way. Afterwards one can be left with a sense of life's mystery and an awe of the previously unknown. But just the opposite can happen—an increase of fear that something similar will happen again.

Krishnamurti (1980) reminds us that there are conscious and unconscious fears. Unconscious fears are the more difficult to recognize and control. Most of the time we live with them. But a crisis can catapult deep fears into consciousness. This has its advantages, for those fears must be confronted if a person is to mature. That is why, he explains, that in the "flowering (of fear) there is intelligence" (p. 94). We sense this opportunity, he believes, and when we fail to learn from it, we experience despair. Krishnamurti defines despair as one's insufficiency to the opportunity. The result is profound sorrow, without any known cause, leaving nothing to react to, nothing to analyze.

There is a way that Christian thought may be of great solace to many of the bereaved. It can be regarded as having made suffering central to its doctrines. Christ on the cross connects suffering to the divine. This makes Christianity a religion for many sufferers because Christ Himself knew of and addressed the tribulations not just of physical pain but mental and spiritual struggles as well. Though suffering Himself, He did not allow Himself to give in to pity or hate.

SUMMARY

This review reveals how central to the concerns of the bereaved are matters more closely associated with spirituality and religion than with psychology. It is the author's hope that they are explained in language and concepts that are now not so foreign to clinicians as they may have been. Prayer was presented as self-reflection and self-analysis; aspects of religious behavior were linked to finding meaning in life; faith was described as fostering personal growth and individuation; spirituality was seen as fostering relationships. These connections with psychological constructs should not be surprising: some of the authors in this chapter, like Fowler and Stokes, acknowledge their debt to scientists like Erikson, Piaget, Kohlberg, and Maslow. But there is another explanation.

Social and behavioral scientists, philosophers, and theologians address remarkably similar issues—the welfare and continued development of humans. It is time that we see all these points of view as complimentary, enhancing overall knowledge and understanding. This is particularly true of the human state we call bereavement.

One case might illustrate this point. Dale, a man in bereavement care spoke out forcibly against God for having allowed his wife of 15 years to suffer many months from cancer. "If he was going to take her anyway, why did he have to wait for so long? She didn't deserve to linger in so much pain," he explained on several occasions. "I'll have nothing more to do with a God like that," he concluded.

His anger was not only intimidating to others, keeping him from the support they might offer, but it prevented him from examining aspects of his grief that needed to surface and be resolved to enable him to get on with bereavement. We first sought and found psychological and social interpretations. His family experiences provided one source; as the young-est of four kids he was frequently rendered helpless, a feeling that was broadened and intensified when his only brother, the oldest sibling and father-substitute, lay dying after an automobile accident. From then on his mother would lament each family difficulty with the refrain, "if only Jake were alive," constantly reminding Dale of his inadequacies. Helplessness became a life-long issue that influenced his religious views. God as an all-powerful and controlling force worked well when things were going smoothly in his life. But this view left him irritated at other times, and infuriated at the death of his wife. It took him a while to realize the relationship between helpless feelings and the omnipotence he attributed to God—and vice versa.

Did he really believe God could have spared her? Yes, but the doctors could have done more, too. How? If his wife had gone in sooner for a check-up. That was partially his fault; he should have insisted. Gradually he admitted his sense of responsibility, a curious flip-flop. Little by little the issue came into focus. He was able to learn something about how he used helplessness—and the way his image of an all-powerful deity was shaped by and contributed to that tendency—when it was seemingly to his advantage to do so. It was difficult for him to reclaim some sense of personal power by retaking responsibility for his life and getting on with his grieving, but he decided to try.

People have the capability of working through issues such as this that appear during bereavement. But many are too overwhelmed to do it alone. Others, eager for changes, new ideas, new ways of thinking and living, don't know how to accomplish them. Either way, they decide to turn to a professional for help. Part II of this book outlines ways you, the coun-selor, might respond. The focus of the chapters to follow describe ways professionals in clinical settings can better serve the bereaved.

Part II

Assessment and Strategies of Bereavement Counseling

Chapter 5

Relating and Assessing in the Initial Contact

A person or family group seeks your assistance. Someone important in their lives has died and grief overwhelms them. Some have difficulty falling asleep; for others, food has lost its appeal. They are often confused, easily distracted, and some cry without provocation. It may have been several weeks since the funeral and in spite of what friends have told them, time is not healing all wounds. They come to you on their own, or from a recommendation by a physician, visiting nurse, member of the clergy, or other professional. Either way their grief is apparent.

There are others who are not consciously aware of being bereaved. Some are preoccupied with other difficulties that neither they, nor previous professionals attributed to grief. Perhaps alcohol abuse occurs, somatic difficulties appear, or what seems to be clinical depression sets in. There has been a recent death. You suspect, or a colleague who refers them to you suspects, that there is a connection.

Worden (1982) citing Lazare, provides several clues that can indicate a person has not resolved the grieving state:

1. the person cannot speak of the deceased without experiencing intense and fresh grief;
2. a relatively minor loss triggers intense grief reaction;
3. themes of loss come up in other clinical work;
4. the person has not moved the material possessions belonging to the deceased;
5. an examination of medical records reveals that the person has developed physical symptoms like those of the deceased;

Note: Part II of this book was written with the assistance of Mark Scrivani.

6. radical changes are made in life-style, e.g., excluding dear friends;
7. subclinical depression has been exhibited, often earmarked by persistent guilt and lowered self-esteem over a long period of time; or the opposite is shown—a false euphoria;
8. there has been a compulsion to imitate the dead person;
9. self-destructive behaviors have become evident;
10. a phobia is exhibited concerning death or the kind of illness of the deceased.

Where to begin? You will gather some data from a systematic assessment, but just as much basic information or more will be gathered throughout the course of your relationship. This makes it all the more important that you have some kind of assessment outline or "mosaic" in mind that can be a guide for recognizing and classifying information. This can include, but not be limited to: (a) vital data about the client's demographics; (b) the current situation and the client's perceptions of that situation; and (c) a relevant history of the client's behavior, relationships, and attitudes. But first, give your fullest attention to emergencies.

SUICIDE THREATS

Thoughts of personal death—wondering what it would be like, wishing they could join the loved one, fantasizing about what the eventual reunion in the afterlife might be like, and whether the process might not be hastened through suicide—are not far from the minds of many bereaved. Suicide rates are higher among all ages of widows and widowers, for example, than among their married counterparts, elderly men showing the highest figures (Osterweis et al., 1984). As with all other clinical situations, any mention of suicide by clients should be taken seriously.

Counselors should question clients about the details of their suicidal tendencies in order to determine whether they: (a) have detailed plans about the method of suicide, the place, and time; (b) have begun to give away precious objects and say good-byes; (c) have already taken the necessary preliminary steps such as purchasing a gun. When there is sufficient evidence that the act may be imminent, suicide crisis therapy should immediately be initiated.

Overt suicidal ideations are only one expression of morbid thoughts among the bereaved. Practitioners need to be alert to other signs of death wishes such as attitudes of despair, hopelessness, ennui, or spiritual exhaustion. These could indicate an indifference to living that is thought to hasten death in unknown ways. Mortality figures for the bereaved are higher than among their married counterparts, especially among widowers up to age 75 (Osterweis et al., 1984). This is most marked during the first year of bereavement.

PHYSICAL DIFFICULTIES

Early in the assessment clinicians should question their clients about their general health, how they are caring for ailments, and from whom they are receiving medical or nursing care. If there are doubts or questions about their physical condition, practitioners should strongly recommend a physical examination. At appropriate times, clinicians may consider seeking or exchanging information with the physician.

Parkes (1987–1988) sees that the damaging effects of bereavement on physical health are now well documented. Stroebe and Stroebe (1987) find that widows and widowers have higher rates of physical disorders than married couples of the same ages. Frederick (1985) maintains that the appearance of cancer after an intense loss has been reported too often to be mere coincidence. These conditions are due most likely to physiological changes produced directly by the bereavement state, the effects of the stress that accompanies grief, or the changes produced by less active, often less healthy life-styles adopted during bereavement.

Raphael (1977) cites a pattern of health deterioration among widows that includes sleeplessness, general nervousness, excessive tiredness, depression, increased drug use, and lessened ability to work. A study she conducted of intervention/nonintervention groups showed that the latter displayed significantly greater frequencies of the following characteristics: swollen or painful joints and general aching, feelings of panic and excessive sweating, excessive tiredness, weight loss, increased smoking, and increased alcohol intake.

Osterweis et al. (1984) remind us that some ailments such as bodily complaints seem to predominate in specific ethnic and occupational groups. They label this phenomenon "culturally approved somatization of bereavement," (p. 205) adding that it makes it particularly difficult for health providers to identify and respond effectively.

PSYCHIATRIC DIFFICULTIES

There are other forms of destructive behavior that occur in bereavement. Ferguson, Schorer, Tourney, and Ferguson (1981) report four observable patterns from their studies of widowhood that signal difficulties: (a) brutalization, meaning the bereaved take out their feelings of anger and guilt on another person; (b) victimization, where the bereaved allow themselves to be the target of others' anger and/or to be controlled by others; (c) self-brutalization, where the bereaved abuse themselves; and (d) insulation, where they withdraw from the outer world.

If the client exhibits behavior and attitudes that lead the clinician to suspect a psychiatric condition, and especially if a previous psychiatric condition is revealed, it is imperative that either (a) intensive therapy be initiated, or (b) a referral be made for further assessment or therapy. It is important, however, that the client's bereavement be acknowledged and care provided.

MAKING THE ASSESSMENT

As soon as emergency conditions, if present, have been alleviated, the assessment that every professional makes of the client's circumstances and condition can be undertaken. The purpose of the assessment is to (a) provide basic demographic data; (b) gather information necessary for judging the severity of the client's bereavement condition, setting goals, and making other decisions concerning the service to be offered; and (c) detect the outline of the individual or individuals who stand before you.

The principles and basic procedure of assessment need not be reiterated here. There is, however, specific information that is relevant to the bereavement state that should be considered in most cases.

Assessing the Severity of the Client's Bereavement

How can the severity of the client's bereavement be determined? Significant symptoms must be identified. These include the following (which are not arranged in any order of priority or intensity):

- the time it takes for grief to appear;
- the duration of bereavement;
- the intensity of symptoms;
- the presence and characteristics of perceived supports;
- the characteristics of the client's relationship with the deceased;
- the degree of disruption in the religious/spiritual dimensions.

Each of the first five symptoms can be assessed by the therapist and arrayed along a continuum of intensity, using Worden's classifications (1982) of normal, difficult, and pathological mourning as benchmarks (see Table 5.1); the sixth, the characteristics of the client's religious and spiritual life, will be handled separately. A continuum appropriately depicts the fluidity and imprecise nature of bereavement in a way that categories cannot. Each of the six symptoms must be discussed in more detail in order to better distinguish among them.

The Time It Takes for Grief to Appear. As indicated in previous chapters, there is widespread agreement that when grieving symptoms do not appear soon after the death of someone significant a signal flag should be raised. Still, not everyone agrees. Wortmann and Silver (1989) write, "available evi-

Table 5.1. Therapist's Form for Assessing Bereavement States[a]

Symptoms	Normal	Difficult	Pathological
1. The time it takes for grief to appear			
2. The duration of bereavement			
3. The intensity of symptoms			
4. The presence and characteristics of perceived supports			
5. The characteristics of the client's relationship with the deceased			

[a]The therapist should fill in relevant information in the appropriate columns.

dence provides little support for the assumption that those who fail to experience distress shortly after loss will have difficulties later" (p. 351). It behooves clinicians, however, to be safe and to not dismiss the person who has recently experienced a major loss as being free of difficulties—especially if that person has come in search of assistance.

There are a wide variety of reasons people suppress grief. Demi and Miles (1987) discuss the fact that some egos either are not sufficiently developed to cope directly with severe losses, or see a given loss as an extension of the self, which compounds the threat and makes it too difficult to face. Many people believe they are not supposed to reveal their feelings—even to themselves. Sometimes survivors realize early after a loss how discomforting their grief can be to those people they must now depend upon; this is especially true for the elderly and handicapped. Families may believe that to show feelings only intensifies and prolongs the pain. Some religions teach that death is a "deliverance" or salvation that should be celebrated, not mourned. Parkes and Weiss (1983) believe that the deterioration of bereavement customs, particularly in Western societies, has discouraged public displays of grief.

Some people encounter financial and other survival problems as consequences of a death, and these may temporarily overshadow the death itself. Grief might be postponed when there are no remains or the griever is not able to view the body for confirmation. Some conditions of death, for example, a painful, mutilating death, death of an infant, death of a new spouse, or a death before bereavement for another is completed, may be too overwhelming to be taken in all at once.

When does postponement or denial become abnormal or pathological? Most people would see as abnormal the responses of the 13-year-old girl who, 8 months after she had seen—and even touched—her dead father, continued to believe that he was alive and would return. As a defense mechanism for a limited period of time, denial can serve a useful purpose. But if prolonged, it can lead to the state Lifton (1982) terms psychic numbing; a diminished capacity to feel. Numbing is a psychic closing off, a way of coping with experiences and images that are too threatening or too overwhelming to absorb or respond to in ordinary ways. Yet Lifton warns that even numbing does not necessarily indicate pathology: there can be selected or partial numbing that sometimes is necessary for someone to function day by day.

As with most other diagnoses, the extreme conditions of normality and pathology in expressing grief are more readily discernible than the middle range behaviors. Nevertheless, the practitioner should flag any case where he or she suspects that the limited display of grief is inappropriate to the severity of the loss.

The Duration of Bereavement. Parkes and Weiss (1983) see three factors that tend to perpetuate bereavement: (a) the nature of the relationship with the deceased, (b) the personality of the survivor, and (c) the surrounding social circumstances.

The nature of the relationship. Obviously the more intense any relationship is, the more difficult will be the loss. But a growing list of studies elaborate on that theme. They find a significant relationship between a previously highly dependent, relatively nondifferentiated (bonded or fused) relationship and prolonged bereavement periods (Raphael, 1983; Rynearson, 1987). Yet ambivalency, too, toward the dead person tends to keep bereavement going (Volkan, 1975). It is not known whether that is because ambivalency aggravates the number and intensity of feelings such as guilt and self-reproach, or whether the ambivalency itself must be resolved along with the bereavement. Bowlby (1980) reminds us that many "healthy" grievers also experience ambivalence toward the lost person.

The personality of the survivor. The personality of the survivor, especially how well he or she is able to cope with stress and stress-related incidents, is an important factor in determining how long a bereavement period will last. Previous psychopathologies such as mania, schizophreniform psychoses, and depression can complicate and prolong grief (Horowitz et al., 1984). Lindemann (1944) concluded that people with an obsessive personality make-up and a history of former depression are likely to develop an agitated depression.

Clinicians will find many other, nonpathological personality features that can prolong bereavement. Being cared for and made the object of much attention can be a heady experience to some. For others, the bereaved state allows them to break with an oppressive life-style that, they fear, will return when they are viewed by others as "cured."

The surrounding social circumstances. The attitudes of family and friends play a significant role in determining the length of bereavement. Lindemann (1944) reminds us, for example, that the readjustment required by the disintegrated social or family system due to the death of a key member may complicate and extend bereavement. Freese (1977) notes other difficulties of adjustment, including changes in residence, establishment of new relationships, expanded or diminished sexual interests, new requirements of work, and changes in attitudes by colleagues.

For some people, whatever the explanation, closure is not reached and the process appears to be feeding on itself, without movement toward resolution. It becomes what is referred to as "chronic" or "unresolved" bereavement. But as noted in chapter 2, there remains considerable confusion among the authorities, as well as the general public, about how long bereavement should run before it becomes dysfunctional. In short, the time line for uncomplicated grief is yet undetermined and seems to grow longer the more the issue is studied (Zisook et al., 1982). Comments like this are forcing clinicians to alter their concept of bereavement resolution from one in which the bereavement process "ends" to one in which the loss no longer dominates the survivor's daily existence. Chronic grief has become much more of a judgment call than it ever was.

The Intensity of Symptoms. There is evidence that, at least for some people, the greater the early intensity of grief, the greater the difficulty of the bereavement adjustment and the more prolonged the bereavement period (Parkes and Weiss, 1983). But how is intensity to be measured?

Lindemann (1944) found nine "distortions" of the grieving process:

- overactivity without a sense of loss;
- symptoms of hypochondriasis or hysteria;
- a group of psychosomatic conditions—predominantly ulcerative colitis, rheumatoid arthritis, asthma;
- alterations in relationships with friends and relatives;
- overflowing hostility directed against specific persons;
- struggle against hostility;
- loss of patterns of social interactions;
- engagement in activities detrimental to the griever's own social and economic existences;
- agitated depression, insomnia, feelings of worthlessness, bitter self-accusation, obvious need for punishment, and thoughts of suicide.

Horowitz and others (1984) identify several common emotional themes that appear after a major loss:

- sadness;
- fear of repetition;
- fear of merger with victim;
- shame and rage over vulnerability;
- rage at the source of the event;

- rage at those exempted;
- fear of loss of control of aggressive impulses;
- guilt or shame over aggressive impulses;
- guilt or shame over surviving;
- guilt stemming from an exaggerated sense of responsibility.

Sadness, the first theme on the list, is the unavoidable reaction to all losses. However, its symptoms are much like those of clinical depression. Rynearson (1987) believes that depression has become "conceptually synonymous" with pathologic grief: It is easy to mistake one for the other, but it is vital that clinicians discriminate between them.

According to Jacobs and Ostfeld (1980), the conditions that resemble depressive illness include the biologic signs of depression such as sleep disturbances, anorexia, weight loss, decreased libido, and diurnal mood variations. Schneider (1984) reminds us that, as difficult as it may be, professionals can distinguish between the deep sadness of normal grief and depression as one of the pathological responses to grief. He presents critical differences in Table 5.2

The Presence and Characteristics of Perceived Supports. Stroebe and Stroebe (1987) see the perceived lack of social support as the single most predictable measure of poor functioning. Some people with only one or two dependable friends may feel better tended to, however, than someone with a host of acquaintances or a large, surrounding family. But as we all recognize, presence of family members is not always helpful. Caroff and Dobrof (1975) remind us that death can be an assault on the family system as well as on the individuals within the group. Relatives may serve as a buffer against stress in some circumstances but amplify the effects of a crisis on other occasions. Reactions of the family unit depend in part on:

- the stage it is in (marital pair stage, child-raising stage);
- the role ascribed to the dead person (scapegoat, great pacifier, family clown);
- the family's ethnic and religious context;
- family myths and history, especially the way they have operated in past crises.

The healthier a family's functioning before the death crisis, the more resources it is likely to have during the current stress (Caroff & Dobrof, 1975).

Characteristics of the Client's Relationship with the Deceased. How can the clinician break through the strong tendency of the bereaved to idealize the loved one, especially when it is buttressed by the custom of speaking only well of the dead? This question gives added importance to the data that will be gathered by taking a history of the relationship. It is important to note

Table 5.2. Key Differences Between Grieving and Depression

	Grieving	Depression
Loss	Recognizable loss by the bereaved.	May be no recognizable loss by the depressed, or it is seen as punishment.
Mood states	Quick shifts from sadness to more normal states in same day; variability in mood, psychomotor activity level, verbal communication, appetite, and sexual interest within same day/week.	Sadness mixed with anger; Tension or absence of energy; consistent sense of depletion, psycho-motor retardation, anorexia with weight loss, sexual interest is down; or there is agitation, compulsive eating, sexuality, or verbal output.
Expression of anger	Open anger and hostility.	Absence of externally directed anger and hostility.
Expression of sadness	Weeping.	Difficulty in weeping or in controlling weeping.
Dreams, fantasies, and imagery	Vivid, clear dreams, fantasy and capacity for imagery, particularly involving the loss.	Relatively little access to dreams; high capacity for fantasy or imagery of a self-destructive nature; severe insomnia, early morning awakening.
Sleep disturbance	Disturbing dreams; episodic difficulties in getting to sleep.	Severe insomnia, early morning awakening.
Self concept	Sees self as to blame for not providing adequately for lost object; tendency to experience the world as empty; preoccupation with lost object of person.	Sees self as bad because of being depressed; tendency to experience self as worthless; preoccupation with self; suicidal ideas and feelings.
Responsiveness	Responds to warmth and reassurance.	Responds to repeated promises, pressure, and urging, or unresponsive to most stimuli.
Pleasure	Variable restrictions of pleasure.	Persistent restrictions of pleasure.
Reaction of others	Tendency for others to feel sympathy for griever, to want to touch or hold the person who is grieving.	Tendency to feel irritation toward the depressed; others rarely feel like touching or reaching out to the depressed.

Note: Reprinted from Stress, Loss, & Grief by J. Schneider, pp. 262–263, with permission of Aspen Publishers, Inc., © 1984.

incidents from this history that seem to be critical turning points in the relationship that should be explored at later times.

The Degree of Disruption in the Religious/Spiritual Dimensions. A person's religious practices and beliefs can be a stabilizing force in a suddenly chaotic life. But the author believes that when these dimensions are disrupted, either prior to a major loss or as one of the consequences, bereavement is intensified and prolonged.

The degree to which religious beliefs and faith are disrupted can range from slight and inconsequential to severe. As with the effects of bereavement, this, too, can be arranged along a continuum as depicted in Table 5.3. A slight disruption, which requires only a few adjustments, would be listed on the extreme left side; severe disruptions, requiring a serious reconstruction of one's faith, would be placed on the opposite end. In between would be placed incidences of questioning and confusion that could lead to partial changes. Those occasions when a person suffered a major loss while passing from one of Fowler's (1981) stages to another would probably be located at the extreme "reconstruction" end. Someone whose faith is strengthened as a consequence of bereavement would be ensconced at the opposite, unquestioning pole.

The author contends that few people, if any, experience a major loss without questioning their faith and beliefs to some extent. Many people experience a crisis of faith, meaning they engage in an emotional, often painful, reconstruction. As stated in chapter 4, this process can continue for years.

The delineations on the religious continuum should not be equated with the three variables listed by Worden (1982) (See Table 5.1). Pathological grief may involve a deterioration of the religious life, or an unsettled religious base may contribute to certain pathological conditions, but until there is more evidence of a relationship, we shall have to treat the two as separate, although possibly interrelated, dimensions.

It is important to remember that one's religious beliefs and faith are demonstrated in both direct and tangential ways. There is little doubt that the widow who suddenly ceases the practice of many years of regularly attending synagogue services, the father who rails against God for taking

Table 5.3. Therapist's Form for Determining Disruption of Religious Beliefs and Faith[a]

	Relatively Unsettled	Unsettled and Questioned	Reconstruction Needed
The characteristics and intensity of the client's religious and spiritual life			

[a]The therapist should fill in relevant information in the appropriate columns.

his son, and the young woman who begins reading about religions different from the one in which she has been raised are experiencing a severe
shake-up in their religious views. But so is the man who resigns his
corporate position to become a social worker, or the woman who surren-
ders the family's second income so she can be at home more often with
the kids.

Those who are practicing members of an organized religion probably
will have more direct ways of explaining their spiritual concerns, using
recognizable terms and phrases. Many others have greater difficulty. Regardless, the clinician must be sensitive to convictions and doubts that are
only dimly understood by the client. These may be expressed symbolically
or through contradictions. For example, a professed atheist hospice patient
once started listing what he liked and disliked about "other people's gods."
He thought he was maintaining his objectivity but the emotional overtones of his "likes" revealed a previously hidden sense of deity.

These deep beliefs most likely will not be revealed in response to per-
functory or passing questions so often asked by professionals. (What is
your church membership? Is religion of importance to you?) The client has
to believe that the interviewer is seriously interested in his or her beliefs
and will not be offended or critical of what is expressed.

Stoll (1979) suggests several questions that can produce valuable spiritual and religious information that, on the surface, seem directed to other
matters.

- Who is the most important person in your life?
- To whom do you turn when you need help? Are they available? In what
  ways do they help you? What happens when you pray or meditate?
- What do you think is going to happen to you?
- Is there anything that is especially frightening or meaningful to you
  now?

If the answers contain no direct reference to a god or a religious group, it
is important to find out why not in later sessions.

There are other ways of determining spiritual beliefs and practices.
Ellerhorst-Ryan (1985) assesses the client's "spiritual distress" using a
questionnaire based on a definition written for the 1980 Fourth National
Conference on Classification of Nursing Diagnoses. She focuses on several
factors: forgiveness, love, hope, trust and meaning, purpose in life, and the
factors necessary to establish and maintain a relationship with God, however "God" is defined. She also provides a way to assess spiritual well-
being, defined as "the affirmation of life in a relationship with God, self,
community, and environment that nurtures and celebrates wholeness"
(p. 95).

Moberg (1984) developed a spiritual well-being scale that questions social attitudes; self-perceptions; theological orientation; activities serving others in charitable, political, and religious contexts; and religious beliefs, opinions, experiences, preferences, and affiliation. He has developed seven indexes identified through factor analysis: Christian faith, self-satisfaction, personal piety, subjective spiritual well-being, optimism, religious cynicism, and elitism. Stoll's (1979) *Guidelines for Spiritual Assessment,* is used to evaluate the ability of hospitalized patients to have their spiritual needs met, but the questions have applicability to the bereaved: 13 questions address a patient's concept of God, sources of hope and strength, religious practices, and the relationship between spiritual beliefs and health.

The clinician who has never before assessed religious and spiritual concerns may at this point feel somewhat overwhelmed at the prospect. But, if given a chance, the client can make your task much easier: Many of the bereaved have been thinking about the topics listed in the above paragraphs, even though they may not have understood them to be "religious."

SPECIAL CONSIDERATIONS

There are several types of clients that may present conditions that deserve special consideration. These are: the conjugally bereaved; different age groups such as children, adolescents, and the elderly; and those influenced by cultures outside the American mainstream.

Conjugal Bereavement

Raphael (1983) sees considerable concurrence in studies from different sources concerning the factors that are relevant to the outcome of conjugal bereavement. Many of these factors—characteristics of the preexisting relationship, the circumstances of the death, and the survivor's social network support—have been mentioned in other contexts. There are other considerations, however, to which the counselor should be alert. These might be revealed by asking some variation of the following questions:

- What was your relationship to your spouse in the beginning? This may help to reveal the overall quality of that relationship and how well or poorly feelings are being resolved. The clinician should note how often the client uses the present or past tense, whether he or she avoids mentioning the deceased by name, the level of emotion that escapes when the spouse is named, how often negative events or qualities are mentioned, and the level of affect that appears.
- How have things been going since the death? A general question like this allows the client to describe his or her perceptions of the quality of present life and what problems need to be faced.

Raphael suggests using data from these and similar questions to draw up a risk profile.

Age Groups

Common sense tell us that clients of different ages will grieve differently. And yet, we must heed Bowlby's (1980) warning that, despite enormously increased attention to the subject, empirical data that differentiate among the reactions of individuals of different ages are scarce. Nevertheless, age differences call for different kinds of data to be gathered.

Children. Bowlby (1980) has found, even among 2-year-olds, marked reactions when separated for lengthy periods from the mother or surrogate mother. These reactions include vigorous searching behavior followed by an emotional withdrawal before a substitute attachment is made. Children's reactions following the death of a parent will be determined by the capacity to form and retain an inner image of the person who has died; this will be based on the development level and capacity for internalization of the child. But there are other factors that influence children's grief:

- the previous kind and level of interaction between the child and the deceased, whether it has been satisfactory or ambivalent;
- the developmental emotional response level;
- the level of cognitive functioning in spheres of causality, time, concrete versus abstract thought;
- the prevalence of magical thinking;
- the degree to which a polarized sense of the good or bad about the experience predominates;
- the actual cognitive understanding of death.

Raphael (1983) adds other factors that influence the outcome of childhood bereavement: (a) the characteristics of the death and whether the child can understand the circumstances, (b) the availability of supportive care, and (c) the extent and intensity of additional stresses in the child's life.

Adolescents. Raphael (1983) sees that for the adolescent, death is an anathema. Their responses to the clinician's questions will reflect the fact that everything in their lives emphasizes living and growth. Their bodies' development, the excitement of their expanding thought processes, the beckoning world of adulthood and power: All these things make death seem unreal. Regardless, many adolescents will face up to and resolve their loss well, even if it takes a long period of time.

The factors influencing the outcome of adolescent bereavement are not much different than those influencing both child and adult responses. In addition, however, further data on adolescent bereavement needs to be gathered, especially information on the nature and quality of family and peer social supports and the number and kind of concurrent crises.

Raphael (1983) also reports that earlier losses, for instance the death of a parent in childhood, may reappear to amplify the grief over another loss in adolescence. This may occur when the adolescent leaves home for college, when a high school romance breaks up, or during the developmental losses that accompany the passage from childhood. These reactions may also be influenced by the growth of concepts of death, evolving security in family life, and the evolution of surrogate relationships. The adolescent has more resources to call upon in bereavement than in childhood, Raphael maintains.

Elderly. Gramlich (1968) believes that the aged grieve differently than the young and middle-aged adults—which could pose special difficulties for the typical young or middle-aged counselor. Kastenbaum and Aisenberg (1972) provides one possible explanation: changes in attitudes about death that occur in late middle age. Gramlich finds a pattern of inhibited yet chronic grief. The most common manifestation of grief in the aged is overt somatic pain and distress. Bereaved elderly patients frequently present themselves to physicians with physical complaints such as gastrointestinal symptoms, and/or joint and muscular pains. It is important, he reminds us, that any history taken by a clinician include questions of previous important losses, with special attention to anniversary dates. Kastenbaum is convinced that the fear of death is not especially intensive or pervasive for the elderly. He believes the majority of them have come to terms with their mortality, which influences how they grieve for others.

Cultural Differences

Osterweis et al. (1984) see that culture exerts a significant influence on the way loss is perceived and experienced. For example, some cultures do not acknowledge illness as part of the postbereavement response; when illness occurs they attribute it to a moral or religious failing. It is important to be aware of both the similarities and variations in the way bereavement is experienced across cultures, ethnic groups, and social classes.

First-generation members of many American minority groups may lack the resources that were available to their parents or grandparents during bereavement. Yet they may not have adopted more mainstream bereavement practices or made use of available resources outside the extended family.

One of the conclusions of McGoldrick et al., (1986) from their study of four cultural patterns (Irish, African-American, Puerto Rican and Chinese) is that therapists must be sensitive to the variety of meanings death can have for families of different cultural backgrounds. Parkes and Weiss (1983) concur, saying that religious and cultural beliefs about death define much of what the bereaved have to accept.

OTHER ASSESSMENT CONSIDERATIONS

Information must be gathered on two important matters: how the client has allowed others to help him or her in the past; and how the patient acts at his or her worst (Gustafson, 1986). This information allows the therapist to determine if the client is a good candidate for brief therapy or whether something more intensive and lengthy is necessary. Furthermore, the clinician can decide if the present crisis is the client's worst or whether he or she has been more disturbed at some other time in life. What was the client like then?

Some therapists prefer to obtain basic assessment data even before the first visit by the use of questionnaires. That way the first session can be spent verifying or refashioning hypotheses formed in advance. Horowitz et al. (1984) warn their fellow clinicians to be prepared for considerable abreactions even during assessments, as emotional reliving of the events take place. These responses will be discussed in chapter 6.

Short- or Long-Term Counseling

Some therapists like to operate through a contract with clients, working out specific objectives with them in the first session, and establishing the probable number of sessions. Other clinicians prefer a more open-ended style. Either way most authorities favor brief counseling unless a pathology is identified that calls for more extensive work (Horowitz et al., 1984; Raphael, 1983; Worden, 1982).

The decision to limit the number of sessions delivers some subtle but important messages to clients: that they are not "crazy" as they may have believed; that the professional has confidence in their underlying ability to cope with the loss; and that the time period for the acute grief stage may be more circumscribed than they first believed. Furthermore, shorter term models help to prevent the counselor from becoming a replacement for the lost person.

Horowitz et al. (1984) believe it is important to announce before the end of the first session the probable length of the relationship. A specific number, he believes, encourages focus and parsimony. But many bereavement counselors prefer to be less structured, arranging the frequency of visits to correspond with the client's needs, and leaving the decision of when to terminate in abeyance. An alternative to termination for some clients is spacing sessions farther apart, like every other week or once a month, perhaps even shifting to an "as needed" basis.

Establishing an Effective Relationship

In addition to those matters already touched upon in establishing an effective relationship between the practitioner and client, we heed Smith's (1982) reminder that the client is sizing you up, just as you are assessing him or her; and may be concerned about how warm, patient, and ready you are to help, whether the two of you are likely to have any common ground for understanding each other, your possibly different world views, and whether you can actually communicate.

We must remind ourselves that both the person being helped and the helper are operating out of inner images, partly conscious and partly unconscious, of the role of helper and the one being helped. Is seeking help a sign of weakness? Do only pathological grievers or those experiencing difficult bereavement seek help? It helps sometimes to openly confront questions like these so that the images and role expectations both parties bring to the relationship can be reconciled.

It is imperative in bereavement care, as with other forms of professional help, that a safe, secure environment be created for the client. Raphael (1980) stresses that beginning with the first few words, the helper must show a warm, encouraging demeanor. This encourages the client to get down to the business at hand as quickly as possible.

There is one final task to be accomplished before the first session ends: arrangement of fees. Many clients expect the services to be donated. In turn some professionals also find it difficult to charge for bereavement care; "It makes me feel I am taking advantage of an unfortunate human condition," one therapist reported. If clients honestly cannot afford a fee, even one adjusted to their income level, or refuse payment, most communities have some kind of volunteer bereavement program to which they may be referred. But clients should understand the differences between the care they could have received from the professional services and what is available from volunteers.

SUMMARY

Do not be surprised to discover that many of those in bereavement who come to you seek not "therapy" but a warm, caring relationship, regardless of how temporary, and a few words of clarification and support. You, the clinician, may be able to provide this in a single visit. But you must be prepared to perform professional tasks as well.

By the end of the initial interview, you should be able to: (a) make at least a tentative decision about the degree of complexity of the client's bereavement, (b) find the focal issues, and (c) outline or sense a counseling or therapeutic plan. After tending to whatever emergencies exist, you should seek the information needed to determine whether a referral is needed for more specialized care. In the vast majority of cases clients will require neither emergency nor specialized care. They seek direct and immediate help from you. We now turn our attention to the strategies and approaches that can be used in professional bereavement care.

Chapter 6

Working With the Client

This chapter is divided into several sections: working with those whose bereavement, while otherwise normal, is temporarily exacerbated by fear, confusion, or overwhelming emotions; working with clients having difficult or complicated bereavement; and working with clients experiencing pathological bereavement. A final section is devoted to a brief discussion of psychopharmacological and family therapies.

NORMAL BEREAVEMENT
TEMPORARILY EXACERBATED

Why should a client whose behavior, from the assessment, appears to be within the range of acceptable bereavement reactions seek professional help? For any one of several reasons. The client might believe that his or her reactions are excessive or unnecessarily prolonged, or that the anger and dark thoughts indicate some sort of craziness. Maybe the client's relationships with children or other family members have become difficult. He or she might have grown weary of grief and want help in putting together a different life. Perhaps he or she needs your help because there is no one else to turn to.

You anticipate that your relationship with this person may be too informal or brief to warrant clearly stated goals. But you will be pleased, at the conclusion of your relationship, if the client:

1. is less worried about those aspects of grief that bothered him or her;
2. better understands and is more willing to accept his or her grieving style;

3. better understands the general characteristics of how humans respond to loss;
4. is better able to continue his or her bereavement.

Informal Counseling

The foundation of informal bereavement counseling, indeed even of more sophisticated therapies, is (a) providing empathic, compassionate support, and (b) empowering the bereaved to successfully process their grief. The first of these requirements seems to run counter to one of the main tenets of professional care—dispassionate service. But it is the bereaved's pain and confusion that must be acknowledged and tended to before much else can transpire.

Because informal counseling is time constricted, the strategies available to the professional are limited. Essentially they can be grouped into three categories: (a) empathic listening, (b) education, and (c) problem solving.

Empathic Listening. As stated elsewhere, the bereaved need to tell their stories, to explore the meaning of the lost relationship, and to place these in a personal historical perspective. Most grievers will readily talk about themselves, their relationship with the deceased, and their present circumstances. If they are reluctant there are several devices that might be used:

- looking together through photograph albums and examining mementos from their past, such as seashells from a seashore vacation or programs from sporting events;
- having them fill out the "Personal Grieving Style Inventory" (Appendix A) and reviewing responses together;
- having them write a letter to the deceased and discussing that together.

Exercises like these help to clarify the boundaries between past and present and provide opportunities for clients to show anger, sadness, and other feelings.

It is important that the bereaved express their grief without fear of being judged or made to feel unusual. The bereaved can be very sensitive to the reactions of listeners, instantly becoming aware of embarrassment, shock, boredom—or the opposite—compassion and empathy. A few honestly shed tears or other expressions of feelings by the clinician affirm the client's own emotions better than words—sometimes with more comfort. But remember: clinicians must keep their emotional responses within reasonable bounds so that the focus is not shifted away from the client.

Do you make physical contact with clients to console them? Many agencies have strict regulations prohibiting touching of any kind because there are risks. (These are discussed in more detail in chapter 7.) However, if you are someone who naturally reaches out to console or celebrate by touching, consider doing this in your work with the bereaved. Remember to remain sensitive to the clients' reactions and to your motivations. If you are in doubt about a client's reactions, ask in advance if he or she minds being touched.

Because you may see these bereaved clients only a few times, issues of transference and counter-transference should not arise. Do not be surprised, however, if you both form quick attachments with each other. Grief can easily bond people together.

Education. Clients frequently will ask, "Is there something wrong with me?" Perhaps friends or adult children have said they are grieving too much or too long. The bereaved frequently need authoritative information regarding what grief is all about.

Data from the literature is valuable, but even more helpful is information conveyed in a personal context. Grievers are attentive to other grievers—who by testimony and display of their feelings—become the most reliable authorities. That is why bereavement groups can be so helpful. In a one-on-one situation, the clinician can substitute by disclosing some of his or her own grief experiences. The counselor must be cautious, however, not to substitute personal interpretations of grief for what is verifiable in the literature. It is easy for grievers to believe that their idiosyncratic behaviors are universal.

Self-disclosure also provides the client with modeling behavior, thereby legitimizing much of his or her own grief reactions. If the counselor admits to past feelings of confusion, for example, it can not only verify for the client that those feelings are natural but also allows the griever to better understand that these are temporary states.

Problem Solving. The problems confronting the bereaved for which they seek assistance might be interpsychic, interpersonal, spiritual, or logistical. There can be questions about whether or not to move to a new location, how to handle the deceased's possessions, whether to seek new friends or break off with relationships that have become unsatisfactory, or how to respond to work demands. Frequently the bereaved need to have options laid out for them and to be helped in exploring the relative benefits of each. This should be done in ways that enhance their personal powers, that is, by clarifying issues and possible courses of action, not by proffering solutions.

Referring the Client

If the griever reveals more difficulties than you originally detected, it is clear that more intensive and sophisticated counseling should be initiated or a referral made to another professional service. On the other hand, if the bereaved's difficulties have been easily resolved, or for other reasons it is not possible or desirable to continue therapy, yet the client still seeks support, the referral can be made to some self-help groups in the community—if they exist—or to church communities that are prepared to help people in grief.

Terminating Relationships

It is sometimes not easy to terminate even a brief bereavement counseling relationship, especially if the relationship has developed into a caring, helpful one. It can be difficult for counselors to turn off their caring for someone who still has much painful grieving to do. But if the original clinical goals have been reached, keeping the clients on your rolls cannot be justified. Besides, neither you nor anyone else can complete the grieving; clients must do that for themselves. (The issue of disengagement is discussed more fully in the final chapter.)

Some counselors have found it helpful to maintain a less intensive form of contact with the client for awhile. A telephone call from time to time or a brief visit the next time the client checks in at the agency, or when the clinician is in the same neighborhood, provides an opportunity to determine if the bereavement period is "going well." These acts also demonstrate continued caring support. Brief notes or cards at anniversaries or other important dates serve similar purposes.

The question of how long to provide help to a griever often is resolved by clients. For some it is useful to arrange sessions on an "as needed" basis, letting them decide when, and for how long, professional help is needed. Sometimes a single session is sufficient for them to develop the perspective they need. Professionals should not assume as a consequence that either they or the clients have failed.

Termination should be carefully planned. If the final visit can be arranged in advance, take time to clear up unfinished business. The client should be encouraged to express any lingering feelings of dissatisfaction and be given the opportunity to express appreciation.

DIFFICULT OR COMPLICATED BEREAVEMENT

How can professionals help people whose bereavement is complicated because of: (a) their inability to initiate or to proceed naturally through the process, (b) their inability to terminate grieving, or (c) the unusual or unnatural circumstances of the death being grieved? Worden (1982) believes that the bereaved demonstrating any one or more of these complications can benefit from bereavement counseling. By this he means a more systematic and extensive relationship between a client and clinician than the informal counseling described in the first section. Bereavement counseling is much more complex and intense and requires the attention of a clinician who has been prepared to work with the bereaved.

Goals

Specific goals, or objectives, must be identified for each case. But these emerge from and must be consistent with general goals for bereavement counseling. Eight statements are offered as a framework to use in shaping goals for individual clients. At the termination of the counseling, through statements in discussions, through accounts of actions and decisions, or by face-to-face behavior, the client will demonstrate some or all of the following behaviors, attitudes, and learnings.

1. **Increased knowledge about the human state called grief and bereavement.**

   It helps for the client to learn what authorities in the field define as typical grieving behavior.

2. **Greater awareness of the way he or she responds to losses, that is, the individual grieving style.**

   Responses to each loss are a composite of reactions to previous losses and present conditions. A client's awareness increases to the extent that the griever is able to recall and understand past responses and reflect on current circumstances.

3. **Emotional expression within a range (a) typical of past responses to situations or events of comparable intensity, and (b) functional for the perceived seriousness of the current loss.**

   For some clients counseling will enable them to better express sorrow, guilt, anger, or other emotions that grief can produce. For others their emotional responses will be toned down through ventilation, control, revised perceptions, or by taking appropriate actions that mitigate bothersome situations. The emotional condition that dominated their lives in the early stages of grief will reflect a better balance after counseling.

4. **A loosening or removal of the blocks or diversions that previously prevented the process of bereavement to run its course.**

   Whatever bonds have tied the client to the deceased will be loosened and the loss acknowledged, both intellectually and emotionally. Tendencies for the development of morbid, dysfunctional bereavement will be reduced.

5. **Increased use of supporting relationships.**

   Relationships with family members and/or friends will be clarified, deepened, and rendered more functional; new supportive relationships will be cultivated. A stronger tie to and image of community will emerge.

6. Strengthened self-confidence and self-image.

Rising from the debris of fears, self-deprecation, and self-punitive attitudes and behaviors will appear a new sense of self that helps to develop and make more effective use of personal resources.

7. Greater awareness of and acceptance of reality.

A new perspective emerges based on greater understanding of the consequences of the client's loss, and a new acceptance of self will develop.

8. Strengthened sense of purpose in and commitment to life, and connection to an ultimate source of life—God, cosmic spirit—however this is defined.

Life, which in the beginning of bereavement was confused and seemingly purposeless, assumes greater direction, and a sense of peace and a love for self and others develops.

Strategies to Employ

A variety of counseling strategies can be adapted to help clients with complicated grief. The ones that have specific applicability to bereavement counseling will be discussed here. Clinicians, though, are encouraged to select from among their personal repertoire those approaches in which they have confidence and that seem best fitted to specific client goals. There are, however, two cautions: first, the strategies selected must be appropriate for the diagnosed bereavement condition; secondly, and following Schneider's (1984) warning, be sure that the techniques employed are not selected primarily to help you, the clinician, feel more useful.

As with informal counseling, and regardless of whatever strategies are used, it is important that empathy and compassion undergird the professional relationship. This means that, as Schneider reminds us, counselors should at times step outside the clinical role, to listen, be available, and "feel" along with the bereaved.

Crisis Intervention Strategies. The crisis intervention approach is "generic" to the treatment of grief, Rynearson (1987) maintains. It focuses particularly on the enhancement of self-esteem, the lessening of anxiety, the expression of emotions, and the strengthening of human supports (goals 3, 4, and 5).

The techniques of crisis intervention are well known and need not be reiterated here. Clients are encouraged to ventilate emotions and reveal thoughts they regard as onerous, in order to air confusion and conflicts. But acute grief has strong regenerative powers. Counselors should not be surprised if the client returns week after week with the crisis seemingly at the same level of intensity. Professionals need to remember that bereavement must run its course at its own pace. Crisis intervention strategies appear to be most beneficial when used in conjunction with other approaches.

An Educational Approach. Gerald Caplan, in the foreword of Glick et al. (1974) observes that the widows in their study benefitted when reassured of their own normality. He found effective the practice of providing each with (a) a rough map of the ground she might have to cover in her struggles to readjust, (b) information about the situations other widows have faced and how they dealt with them. These benefits can be extended to all the bereaved.

Educational strategies can be employed in all counseling and therapeutic situations, whether or not they are the principal model used. Educating, however, is not simply the imparting of information and knowledge. According to Gowin (1981), it is the process by which humans come into possession of the powers of their intellect, emotion, imagination, and judgment. It mobilizes personal resources for active thought and behavior and connects experiences and insights, thereby overcoming feelings of separation and isolation.

In this form of educating, the emphasis is on what the client learns, not what the professional teaches. In counseling situations considerable incidental learning occurs: from the nonverbal as well as verbal reactions of the professional, what the professional discloses about his or her own grief reactions, and conscious and unconscious modeling. The best teacher though, is the client, who gains insights through review and analyses of personal situations and past behavior. The clinician should give instruction or share knowledge when the client, through questions or other cues, demonstrates receptivity.

As in informal counseling, the bereaved can benefit from the personal experiences shared by the clinician. Some may prefer knowledge generalized from authorities in the field. The authors have found that a mixture of the two generally is the most effective way of helping the client find new meaning from experiences.

The Worden Approach. Worden (1982) offers guidelines and specific strategies for grief counseling. He relies heavily upon cognitive and emotional processing. Ten principles are given:

1. Help the survivor actualize the loss;
2. Help the survivor to identify and express feelings;
3. Assist the survivor to live without the deceased;
4. Facilitate emotional withdrawal from the deceased;
5. Provide time to grieve;
6. Interpret "normal" behavior;
7. Allow for individual differences;
8. Provide continuing support;
9. Examine defenses and coping systems;
10. Identify pathology and make a referral, if necessary.

Worden's counseling techniques encourage the client to present a history of the lost relationship, to express feelings, and to deal with present and future circumstances, e.g., forming new relationships, taking on a sexual partner, and moving to a new location. Worden understands that counseling can be beneficial at any time, even prior to the death of the loved one. But he recommends avoiding the time surrounding the event itself, during the shock phase. (I am aware of one recorded case, however, when the client asked to be seen on the day of her son's death.) Where does Worden see the clients? Not necessarily in an office; sometimes he meets them in hospitals or at their homes.

Raphael's Cognitive Approach. Raphael (1983) details a cognitive approach to bereavement counseling that entails the following types of verbal interactions:

- discussing the relationship with the deceased from the beginning. This may reveal the quality of the relationship, level of ambivalence or dependence, and problems of resolution of feelings.
- reporting of what has been been happening since the death to see how things are going. This allows for the quality and extent of other relationships, and the way family and friends block or encourage grieving to be revealed.
- questioning whether the client has been through other bad times recently or when he or she was young.

These discussions are designed to facilitate and enhance an evolving bereavement and to provide a framework for preventive interventions with those who are at risk of developing pathological conditions.

Raphael sees the counseling relationship developing quickly as the client seeks to attach to a supportive person. The bereaved can be highly motivated to seek help. A lowered defensiveness at this time allows for a free flow of material and expression of affect. Often unresolved earlier losses appear, but several types of resistances can surface as well: clients may (a) deny that there are difficulties after all, (b) change the focus of their concerns to something less troublesome, (c) become preoccupied with other people's pain, (d) search for a replacement relationship; (e) introduce a fascinating psychopathology to mislead and divert the counselor. Fears of disintegration, loss of control, and breakdown frequently interfere with the clients' emotional expression.

A Multimodal Format. Proulx and Baker (1981) have designed a multimodal approach that may be used both in classroom and clinical settings for the bereaved. The learner or client is asked to identify, interpret, and distinguish the modalities of Behavior; Affect (the feeling tone expressed); Sensation (the sensory or physical component of grief); Imag-

ery (the mental pictures or memories); and Cognition (the thought processes).

The BASIC model is essentially a problem-solving tool that gives
specification of problems or goals and treatment techniques designed to
address those goals, and an ongoing evaluation of the effectiveness of
treatment.

Educational Models for Faith Development. Examples of therapeutic procedures
that may be useful in helping someone reconstruct his or her religious life
during bereavement are difficult to find. (See the instruments cited in
chapter 5.) Two models designed essentially for pastoral counseling are
cited here. The first is found in *Faith Development and Pastoral Care* (Fowler,
1987) (see Appendix B), and the second in *Heads of Heaven, Feet of Clay*
(McCollough, 1983).

Both of these approaches are based on the Fowler (1987) theory of faith
development briefly described in chapter 4. They present a series of exercises designed to assist clients in reshaping aspects of their perceptions and
interpretations of their religious and spiritual histories. For example, as a
way to help people understand how beliefs and religious values may
change over time, Fowler has participants review their lives from birth to
the present to identify such features as "key relationships," and "uses and
directions of the self." McCollough provides three different frames for
analyzing clients' histories: self-affirmation (the inward journey); self-
giving (the inward and outward journey); and self-extension (the outward
journey). Fowler suggests ten different steps for each client to follow in the
exercise, "The Unfolding Tapestry of My Life"(Appendix B).

Both McCollough's and Fowler's exercises serve two primary purposes:
as starter engines for those whose religious lives have lain somewhat
dormant during their adult years; and as road maps for those who are more
active spiritually and religiously. Both authors acknowledge that any kind
of exercise with another person can be only an aid; the important tasks of
formulating religious beliefs and faith commitments must be done ultimately by each individual within himself or herself.

These and other spiritual journey exercises are most helpful in bereavement counseling when used with other counseling strategies. Spiritual journeys can help grievers to focus on aspects of their lives that may
not have been uppermost in their minds because of the lost relationship.
They provide reminders of other aspects of the world, as well as other
people, to which they are connected. Grievers can review previous life
crises and how they responded to them—and what benefits accrued as a
consequence. A perspective can emerge from these reflections that provides a balance in feelings and images, especially if it continues the self-
reflection through diaries and interactions with others individually and
in groups.

Referring and Terminating Treatment

Clients who reveal complexities during counseling that were not originally diagnosed should be referred to psychotherapeutic or psychiatric specialists. It is not always easy to locate psychotherapists knowledgeable about grief. This is important because regardless of what other personality or system pathologies need to be treated, the client's grief must be tended to as well.

Schneider (1984) sounds additional warnings about referring clients for therapy. The training and orientation of most therapists, he maintains, is focused on abnormal behavior. This can lead to misunderstandings of grieving reactions. Even if the diagnosis is accurate, he fears the consequences of psychotherapeutic "overkill"; the level of technical skill of most therapists may not be necessary in aiding the grieving. Counselors also must be careful not to refer clients in such a way that will raise unnecessary anxieties.

When it is ascertained that continued counseling for a given client can no longer be justified, but he or she nevertheless expresses a desire for continued support, a referral to a self-help group may be appropriate. This step also may be considered after one or two sessions for clients whose condition turns out to be less complicated than originally assumed. It is recommended, however, that counselors telephone former clients a week or so later to obtain their reactions to the group they selected. Self-help programs vary considerably both in their approach to bereavement support and in the quality of their programs. This follow-up call also can reassure clients of the counselor's original concern.

All the techniques described in this section are designed for short-term counseling. The end comes all too quickly for some clients. An alternative to abrupt termination is to extend the period between visits from once a week, to once a month or less frequently. Contact can be maintained in between visits, if desirable, by occasional telephone conversations.

When the counselor is convinced the relationship should be terminated, he or she should apprise the client in advance to obtain a reaction. The bereaved are highly sensitive to feelings of "being abandoned," to unmet dependent needs, and to unfinished relationship issues. As noted earlier in this chapter, attachments between clients and counselors can form quickly. It is important to recognize and deal with these feelings. The contractual arrangement, noted earlier, is one way to forestall these difficulties. Even so, the termination should be carefully prepared, especially if the client's other supports are not yet firmly in place.

All that was said in the informal counseling section about physical contact applies as well to more formal counseling. Because the relationship can extend over a longer time period, embracing and other forms of touching can intensify transference and counter-transference tendencies. Still, grievers in counseling can benefit from hugs. Whether or not to touch a client in any way must be decided on an individual case basis.

PATHOLOGICAL BEREAVEMENT

When pathological bereavement is diagnosed, therapy is appropriate. The purpose of grief therapy, according to Worden (1982), "is to identify and resolve the conflicts of separation which preclude the completion of mourning tasks in persons whose grief is absent, delayed, excessive, or prolonged" (p. 65). Schneider (1984) defines a pathologic reaction as one that "exceeds the capacity of the person to self-correct" (p. 261). The goals detailed for counseling can be used as well for grief therapy to which the objectives of specific therapies must be added.

Strategies of Bereavement Therapy

Therapists, like counselors, are encouraged to adapt to bereavement care those strategies that they are familiar with and use successfully in other circumstances. Nevertheless, they should consider those approaches devised specifically for grief work from which they might select and integrate component parts into their own work.

Several therapies designed for pathological grief are reported in the literature. Schneider (1984) identifies many other therapeutic methods available for use with grievers. Existential psychotherapy, gestalt, psychosynthesis, focusing, bioenergetics, interpersonal process recall, microcounseling, crisis interventions, and ego analytic approaches are but a few of the methodologies that can aid in restoring the natural grieving process. We shall select for description only some of those that have been specifically designed for grief or that have particular relevance to grief therapy.

Worden's Grief Therapy. Worden (1982) begins each case by assessing which of his four grieving tasks have not been completed (accepting the reality of the loss, experiencing the pain, adjusting to an environment in which the deceased is missing, and withdrawing emotional energy and reinvesting it in another relationship). He then selects from and adapts the following goals to the client's specific needs for:

- reviving memories of the deceased;
- dealing with the affect or lack of affect stimulated by memories;
- exploring and defusing linkages to the dead;
- acknowledging the finality of the loss;
- dealing with the fantasy of life without grief;
- saying the final good-bye.

Worden uses a variety of techniques that include role playing, using linking objects and photos, the empty chair technique, and other ways of getting the client to talk to the deceased.

Worden claims that the therapist provides the social supports necessary for all successful grief work. He is often the one who gives the patient permission to grieve. To do this an effective therapeutic relationship must be established. He warns that the client can offer much resistance.

Except for crisis situations when he may begin treatment at the site of the crisis, such as the hospital, Worden (1982) believes that grief therapy should be conducted in an office; about eight to ten visits are the rule. This is usually sufficient time to work through unresolved grief, barring unusual complications. The neurotically dependent personality is one of those exceptions that require expert psychotherapeutic intervention to deal with both the legitimate grief reactions and the underlying personality disorder.

Worden notes that certain special types of losses may require special attention, e.g., suicide, survivors of sudden deaths; parents whose children died from Sudden Infant Death Syndrome (SIDS), still births, or miscarriages; women who have an abortion; and people who are experiencing anticipatory grief.

Regrief Therapy. Volkan's (1975) "regrief therapy" is designed to help the client to remember and reexperience at some point after the critical death, the circumstances surrounding that experience. Its purpose is to help the client accept present circumstances, thereby freeing him or her from the ties to the dead.

Volkan uses this approach when, at least 6 months after the death, he finds intense grief mixed with ambivalence toward the dead one. If the client intellectually acknowledges the loss but does not display the appropriate emotional responses it leaves the clinical state, he maintains, "highly crystallized"; evidence of pathological grief usually manifests itself soon after treatment is begun.

Volkan uses several techniques:

1. the use of "linking objects"; clothing, mementos, photographs, the special tokens of the deceased kept by the bereaved as a way of stimulating memories. The client is asked to touch them and reflect on their meaning as a way of leading him or her into a review of the circumstances before and after the death. Volkan has found that anger usually appears at that point, at first directed toward others, including the therapist, then toward the dead. Abreactions, the emotional reliving of the events, also may occur during these reviews. He encourages clients to take responsibility for negative feelings such as death wishes and deep guilt.
2. tough questioning of contradictory perceptions, such as when a client

intellectually, but not emotionally, accepted the prognosis of the spouse's terminal illness.
3. examination of dreams and fantasies.
4. full acknowledgement of the loss and its meaning, during the final phase of treatment. Volkan recommends trips to the grave for some clients and even has gone along on some on these trips.

Regriefing is short-term but intensive therapy. Volkan will see clients as often as four times a week. This promotes transference, an issue he sees as important to confront.

Grief Resolution Therapy. Melges and DeMaso (1980) have developed an approach they call "grief resolution therapy." It is designed to remove the blocks preventing resolution of grief by the use of abreactive processes. They list nine obstacles to be removed:

1. persistent yearning for recovery of the lost object;
2. overidentification with the deceased;
3. the wish to cry or rage at the loss coupled with an inability to do so;
4. misdirected anger and ambivalence toward the deceased;
5. interlocking grief reactions;
6. unspoken but powerful contacts with the deceased;
7. unrevealed secrets and unfinished business;
8. lack of a support group and alternative options;
9. secondary gain or reinforcement from others to remain grief stricken.

Melges and DeMaso plan for three interrelated phases involving the following techniques:

1. cognitive structuring emerging from regrieving. They first acknowledge the difficulties faced by the client. Then they have him or her describe some pleasant memories of the deceased, encouraging a reexperience of the feelings in those incidents. The client must be helped to discover what parts of him or herself still rest with the deceased so these can be released.
2. guided imagery for reliving, revising, and revisiting scenes of the loss. Melges and DeMaso explain guided imagery as the use of the "mind's eye." The client is asked to describe past events by using present tense verbs and speaking as if events were happening at that time. They structure this review by using questions such as, "The news of X's death just arrived; how do you react?"
    The therapist sometimes revises these events, asking clients to relive past situations with certain persons removed, circumstances altered, or dialogues changed. The client is also encouraged to talk to the deceased.
3. future-oriented identity reconstruction. Clients are asked to imagine

situations 1 year hence, such as standing at the grave or revisiting old haunts.

Meges and DeMaso use grief resolution therapy in conjunction with other therapies. They find, however, that the client's decision to regrieve is therapeutic in itself. How much time is devoted to the regrief work depends on the clarity of the patient's decision, her or his ego-strength, and the extent of the bonds with the deceased. Usually, it requires 6 to 10 half-hour or hourly sessions, which are carried out as focal treatments within the context of other types of therapy.

They warn that grief resolution methods are emotionally draining for therapists. Cotherapists should be considered.

Stress Response Syndrome Therapy. There are several types of therapies for stress response syndrome (SRS), but one devised by Horowitz et al. (1984) seems very appropriate for clients with pathological grief. Stress response syndromes are reactions to serious life events such as recovery from life-threatening circumstances. Clients exhibit SRS through emotional numbing, avoidances of anxiety-provoking situations, and inhibitions of many otherwise ordinary behaviors.

The treatment Horowitz et al. prescribe for those with SRS encourages the client's review of stored information about the recently experienced death. The treatment aims to facilitate adjustment to the experience by bringing about a gradual, in-depth contemplation of the personal implications of the event. They usually limit their therapy to 12 sessions.

Not everyone is suitable for brief therapy, they warn. The most important criterion for selection is the patient's willingness to change. They see this attitude as one that leads to "growth," rather then mere "recovery." For those who would rather be reassured, or just have their emotions toned down, fewer than 12 sessions may be required.

Special care must be taken by the therapist as the agreed upon end point approaches, so that the termination not be misinterpreted by the patient. The patient may feel rejected because he or she hasn't somehow measured up to the therapist's standards. If the patient has not accomplished all that he hoped, this should be discussed—along with other aspects of separation, for example, issues of abandonment. The patient's accomplishments also should be acknowledged both by the client and the therapist. The authors suggest that the issue of termination be raised by the eighth session in order to provide plenty of time to deal with these reactions. This also helps the therapist and client to pace themselves.

Focal Therapy. Raphael (1983) describes the conditions of "focal therapy." This approach is based on an assessment of the particular form of pathological bereavement exhibited by each client. The goal is to convert these

dysfunctional responses to more normal patterns of grief. More specifically, it aims to correct three pathological conditions:

Inhibited, suppressed, or absent grief. The griever explores reasons why death
cannot be accepted and why the emotional states of dependence, guilt, and
fear of bereavement cannot be expressed. Raphael seeks to uncover the
bereaved's defenses to the loss. In a variety of ways the therapist:

- acknowledges the client's pain;
- recognizes that the fears are common;
- recognizes that the defenses serve some purpose;
- recognizes that the client is reluctant to relinquish the dead one and
  helps him or her find the reasons for this;
- recognizes that the client wants to avoid the pain.

Distorted grief. With this form of grief, the client exhibits some extreme
reactions such as anger and guilt but partially suppresses or inhibits other
aspects of grief. Goals are the same as for inhibited grief, and so are many
of the interventions. Often the client in this condition shows a "death
wish" for the dead person. The therapist will have the client analyze the
guilt expressed with such statements as, "I caused the death," or "If only
I had done more," to determine if, in light of actual circumstances, these
responses have any basis in reality.

Chronic grief. This condition can be caused by many circumstances. Certain types of deaths are more difficult to resolve than others, for example,
unexpected deaths and the loss of children. But there are some who experience more typical deaths who also have difficulty in terminating their
grieving. When resolution is delayed for an extended period of time, pathological defenses can become entrenched, perhaps because the client has
gained some temporary advantages as a consequence. Therefore, the client
may not be motivated to seek clarity, that is, the truth, in his or her life.
The client may think, for example, that he or she lacks the personal
qualities needed to attract another mate. Remaining in grief is a way of
avoiding having to face up to and correct that image. Or the client may
suspect that if he or she were to tone down the grief, fantasies about the
past relationship might have to be abandoned, such as that it was not
nearly so ideal as depicted to friends.

The client must explore the meaning of the lost relationship and identify the roles the deceased played, thereby discovering the good and the
bad of what used to be. It is helpful to use a series of concrete tasks, such
as sorting through the dead person's clothing and possessions. These devices are needed, because chronic grievers are a tough group to work with
(Raphael, 1983).

The optimal time for these interventions is 2 to 8 weeks or perhaps as long as three months after the death. Raphael favors six to eight sessions, usually in the bereaved's home. Sessions are often 1½ to 2 hours in length. "Entrenched psychopathologies" should be avoided except when they have specific relevance for the difficulties of bereavement.

Raphael warns the therapist to recognize and accept the fact that regardless of what occurs in the therapeutic relationship, much of the client's grief will be worked out in private or with other supportive family members and friends. The counselor should not attempt to supplant these family and social networks, and, in fact, should help the client to find outside support that may be lacking.

Clinical Art Therapy. Art therapists define the "psyche" as did the ancient Greeks as an integral part of the soul. Many see themselves grounded in depth psychology rather than in behavioral psychology (McNiff, 1989). Art therapists may work with more than one art form, often using music and dance as well. Many different techniques are employed in an attempt to ascertain feelings, meanings, and images lodged in the subconscious. Landgarten (1981), for example, has families make murals together that can reveal not only relationships, but the feeling tone within the groups. Individual drawings, too, can be used for a variety of purposes. She describes the case of an 11-year-old boy who refused to wash; the reason was not determined until his interpretation of drawings revealed that he had been in the shower when he learned of his mother's death.

Other Therapies

Other one-on-one therapies are reported in the literature but, for the sake of brevity, cannot be described in detail. These include three therapies used by Kleber and Brom (1985): trauma desensitization (based on learning theory; using relaxation techniques) in which the patient is gradually confronted with relevant aspects of his loss; hypnosis therapy, which uses hypnosis to confront the bereaved with relevant aspects of loss; and psychodynamic therapy (based on the work of Horowitz), which helps the patient discover and solve interpsychic conflicts related to loss. Lieberman (1978) has devised a treatment that includes a forced mourning procedure based on behavioral principles of systematic desensitization and implosion; this is coupled with family involvement whenever practical. Arkin (1981) developed strategies that have the patient imagine that the dead person, still alive in some way, encourages the griever to develop more mature attitudes and behaviors. Mawson, Marks, Ramm, and Stern (1981) treat unresolved grief like other forms of phobic avoidance and use a guided mourning technique to expose clients to the recent death events. Marmar, Horowitz, Weiss, and Wilner (1988) use brief (12-session), dynamic therapy group techniques aimed at reviewing conflicts involved in the subject's relationship with the deceased spouse.

PSYCHOPHARMACOLOGIC AND FAMILY THERAPIES

Psychopharmacologic Therapies

No aspect of therapy for the bereaved is more controversial than the use of psychopharmacologic interventions. There are three types of medications administered to those in grief: antianxiety drugs (minor tranquilizers and sedatives); hypnotics (sleeping pills); and antidepressants (tricylic antidepressants and monoamine oxidase inhibitors). Should all of these be considered as part of the therapeutic treatment of the bereaved? If so, how often and for what period of time?

Osterweis et al. (1984) maintain that evidence does not support the use of medication to relieve bereavement symptoms. Jacobs and Ostfeld (1980), however, believe there is use for psychopharmacologic medication if it is administered judiciously, such as using sedatives for a short time in the early phases of grief when emotions are excessively high. Hypnotics can be useful for insomnia; antidepressants may be prescribed for intercurrent depressive illnesses that interfere with normal grieving.

While Schneider (1984) notes that alcohol or drugs occasionally help the bereaved to deaden pain, or produce sleep, he discourages their use as a way of coping with loss and grief. The one exception is the use of tricyclic antidepressants. He gives four reasons for his position:

1. drugs cloud the consciousness, distort the intellectual processes, suppress the rapid eye movement sleep cycle, and may even contribute to depressive reactions;
2. clients for whom drugs are prescribed may then become convinced that they are incapable of getting through grief without them;
3. drugs can eliminate pain, which serves as a motivation for getting through grief;
4. writing prescriptions may be most useful for therapists, who feel that they may not be helpful otherwise.

Raphael (1983), too, warns against the use of antidepressants as therapy for normal grief, even though they may be temporarily useful for extreme depression.

Family System Therapies

Death occurs not just for the bereaved partner but for the entire nuclear and extended families. Family-oriented therapy also has been useful in helping the bereaved. It appears that these are for the most part adaptations of approaches used for general family counseling or therapy. In adapting them for bereavement work many factors must be considered.

Raphael (1983) points out that following a death, the roles in each family are redefined for members and the power redistributed based on the perceived needs of individuals and other factors. Proulx and Baker (1981) remind us that the survivors will have varying physical and emotional needs and different levels of intensity of grief, which complicate the task of the counselor. Arkin (1981) suggests that the counselor should focus on the one family member to whom others turn to spontaneously for leadership and support.

Young widows or widowers with children may need special attention (see Fulmer, 1987). They are subjected to an array of stresses from shifts and blending of roles, increased needs of anxious children, and the depletion of family resources. These single parents have to drastically and quickly reshape their own lives at a time when imagination and energy reserves are depleted.

The author has found it helpful to meet with entire families for bereavement care. This practice can (a) improve communication throughout the system, (b) visually and symbolically demonstrate the unity of the group, (c) encourage confrontation with thorny, possibly divisive issues, (d) demonstrate to the therapist and the family itself, some of the changes in relationships taking place because of the death, and (e) help to identify members who need special, individual attention. The home setting is preferred in certain cases to make it easier for all parties to attend.

Who should be invited to these family sessions? Significant members of the extended family should be considered. Some meetings might include a member of the clergy if he or she is playing a significant role during bereavement. Meetings should include special friends or neighbors who sometimes are more important to the nuclear family than relatives who have grown distant. Children and adolescents, especially after the loss of a parent, sometimes benefit from bringing along a best friend for support.

Cotherapists should be considered as the expected group grows in size. This also permits the option at some point in the 1½ to 2-hour sessions for one of the therapists to work separately with an individual or portion of the group.

HOW RELIABLE AND VALID ARE
THESE THERAPIES?

The reader must be reminded of the warning sounded elsewhere in this book, but which has special applicability for this chapter. Among those who review the literature on therapeutic techniques there is considerable hesitation about the soundness of much of the evaluation reported on clinical practices and, therefore, their applicability beyond the cases reported in the literature (Middleton & Raphael, 1987; Osterweis et al., 1984; Parkes, 1987–1988; Rynearson, 1987; Raphael & Middleton, 1987; Wortman & Silver, 1989). Readers are reminded that before they adopt any of the strategies reported in this part of the book they must carefully look at the materials summarized in this chapter to better determine their applicability to other situations.

It is necessary to balance these warnings and dire observations of researchers by remembering how competent counselors and therapists select and adapt ideas proposed by fellow clinicians. As Schön (1983) points out, practitioners do not apply research results reflexively in their work but instead take ideas from a variety of sources (not just research), discard those that seem not to fit, and reshape others. They use a variety of ways to evaluate what works and what does not. This system may be a far cry from what some researchers advocate, and far from the kind of system many psychological practitioners would prefer, but it still enables us to help relieve a great deal of suffering.

Chapter 7

General Principles for Helping the Bereaved

Regardless of the counseling methods selected to help the bereaved, there are many general principles or "rules of the game" to take into account. A review of some of these also provides a summary, but from a different perspective, of some key points presented elsewhere in this book.

ESTABLISHING THE CLIENT–HELPER RELATIONSHIP

The principles for establishing a beneficial relationship with those in grief follow guidelines used successfully for clients with other needs. But certain exceptional conditions should be met.

Grievers, rendered vulnerable by their losses, need to feel protected from further pain. Isolated by many people who are discomforted by grief, they need the attention of a friendly, empathic person. Unable to control their public displays of grief, which at times are humiliating, they need patient acceptance.

It is not easy to establish the right climate: one that offers solace and encourages thoughtful introspection as well as the expression of heavy, explosive emotions. Outbursts of anger and rage, morbid sorrow, and heavy guilt—even the apparent lack of emotion—may be more intense during grief than at any other time in most people's lives.

To create an effective client–helper relationship, it is suggested that the clinician:

- guard against giving dictates and making criticisms, which can add to the clients' feelings of shame, guilt, and self-doubt, while further repressing the expression of these and other feelings;

- recognize, accept, and validate each emotion as it arises so that clients can move on from one feeling state to another;
- be careful not to brush aside, offer platitudes in response to, or judge critically clients' expression of deep-seated fears, doubts, and tumultuous feelings;
- be patient when clients appear to be stuck in their grief.

All these principles assume that the clinician is able to exercise some degree of control in the counseling relationship. There are times when working with the bereaved, however, when it is best to acknowledge a shared helplessness and offer a state of "presence" instead of strength and knowledge. Presence can be defined as being fully with someone who is troubled, projecting the assurance that you will continue to stand by him or her without obligation or complication. It is a quiet acquiescence of things as they are at that moment; a restful pause in an otherwise long, hard climb; a silent moment in the cacophony that is grief. Presence is a powerful, renewing time together. Helpful messages are exchanged by a smile or a touch on the hand.

Touching the Client

As stated elsewhere, to touch or not to touch is a difficult dilemma for many clinicians. Raphael (1983, p. 353) believes that the natural response to the bereaved is "to hold, touch, and murmur sympathy" to them. But as noted in previous chapters, the professional frequently and wisely hesitates, even though she or he knows a hug or a clasped hand can work wonders.

In addition to the reasons for caution already cited in the preceding chapter, clinicians must be sensitive to and honor their own and the client's intimacy boundary lines. The same must be noted for sexual boundaries, especially because some grievers, deprived of sexual relationships for some time and overflowing with so many feelings and needs, find themselves more responsive than usual to tenderness. This can be intensified in one-on-one sessions in private settings. Touching is much less a problem in groups where everyone is hugging and being hugged in public.

Many hospices are remarkable for the way staff members use physical touch so naturally—among themselves and with patients and family members, many of whom are having difficulty touching each other. Frequently, hugging by a staff person encourages them to begin embracing others. Throughout this book clinicians have been urged to be empathic and show compassion. It is important to clarify what this means.

What is Empathy?

Empathy, as used in the helping fields, has essentially three functions: (a) understanding and interpreting another's condition, one person resonating with another; (b) enhancing perceptual scanning and inference, which may include telepathy and matters uncanny; (c) enhancing dispassionate observations essential for uncontaminated understanding of others (Reed, 1984).

Agosta (1984) uses empathy as a form of receptivity and understanding of how another person is feeling. He calls it "vicarious introspection," because it involves experiencing another's experience. This establishes a connection between self and other. Kohut (1984) describes empathy as information-gathering, which, in turn, creates powerful emotional bonds between people.

Goldstein and Michaels (1985), after an excellent review of the literature, conclude that empathy can be defined as the following (p. 7):

- taking the role of the other, viewing the world as he or she sees it and experiencing his or her feelings;
- being adept at reading nonverbal communications and interpreting the feelings underlying them;
- giving off a feeling of caring for, or sincerely trying to understand another person in a nonjudgmental or helping way.

Kohut (1984) rejects the notion held by many that empathy is something sentimental or mystical. He believes that it plays a vital part in therapy helping the therapist to formulate hypotheses and to grasp the client's reactions, and also providing a benefit in and of itself. Our scientific training, Kohut reminds us, has often prevented us from acknowledging the significance of empathy. Shapiro (1984) thinks of empathy as another way of gathering vital data, noting that psychoanalysis relies upon "observations taken by all the senses" (p. 117).

Sympathy, too, consists of having feelings comparable to those being experienced by another. But sympathetic responses are nonobjective, highly personalized, a form of immature empathy. Empathy allows one person to remain detached while experiencing an intimacy with the suffering of another (Olinick, 1984).

What is Compassion?

Precise differentiation between empathy and compassion is not needed for our purposes: both are born from one's own painful experiences, which form the basis for imagining—or reliving—another's suffering. However, there are differences that have relevance to bereavement care. Empathy is more likely to be evoked by and limited to specific situations; for example, the clients are experiencing responses similar to those the professional herself or himself experienced following the death of a parent. Empathy leads to greater sensitivity to situations shared with another person. Compassion is a more generalized state and can lead to a more spiritual way of living in which we treat ourselves, others, and our environment with love. Through compassion we find our most meaningful and emotional maturity. Without compassion, Fox (1979) claims, there can be no change of self, others, or the world. He also maintains that compassion enables professional helpers to enjoy their work more than if they are bound by the orthodoxy of what he terms "control-psychology."

Many clinicians fear that if they show empathy and compassion they will lose control of professional situations. They ask, how can I prevent clients from taking advantage; where will compassion for someone lead? And compassion, many believe, clouds objectivity. These are dangers that all clinicians must be alert to, but experienced bereavement counselors learn to set limits for compassionate behavior and become sensitized to danger signals in their own as well as the clients' responses. Compassion in bereavement care is analogous to comfort for the physically ill; both enhance the conditions that permit, even encourage, change.

THE COMPLEX AND CRITICAL NATURE OF DENIAL

Denial appears so frequently in descriptions of pathological bereavement it deserves additional attention. Although many clinicians think of denial in its extreme form as one of the most telling characteristics of psychoses, Simos (1979) reminds us that "it is the earliest defense to emerge in psychic development, the most persistent of all defenses, and a normal part of ego development. Some denial is necessary at every stage of life to make life bearable for all of us" (p. 60). All the bereaved engage in denial of some sort or other. A new reality must be integrated in bits and pieces. Simos goes on to say that the breaking of any defense is in itself a loss. Premature efforts to remove denial can be risky for the bereaved who already are in a shaky condition. Besides, Simos points out, denial cast off at inappropriate times can quickly be reinstituted.

There are other aspects of denial that must be remembered in grief work. Any uncertainty about the finality of a loss increases denial. Often a client cognitively acknowledges a loss but withholds appropriate feelings. Some people try to quickly replace their losses (by remarrying, becoming pregnant, etc.), believing that grief thereby has been successfully avoided.

EXPRESSING VOLATILE
EMOTIONS

Expressing the emotions of grief, it is believed, helps to keep the bereaved from becoming overwhelmed. But neither the general public nor professionals agree among themselves how much emotional discharge is necessary. Researchers also have failed to establish, as some authors maintain, that there is a preferred sequence in the expression of these feelings, for example, sorrow before anger, or vice versa. No one can predict which feelings will be strongest at any given moment.

Each clinician will have to determine how much and how often each client should be encouraged to express his or her feelings. For a client who constantly cries, for example, the counselor can explain that he or she is willing to spend clinical time this way but that the client, him- or herself, has identified other goals he or she wants to accomplish. Clients who do not express feelings in sessions and admit that they are not emoting in private either may be asked to review details of the death. This provides opportunities for the counselor to observe whether the client appears to be holding back feelings or whether he or she may be one of those persons who do not have deep distressful reactions to grief. If the review reveals emotionally sensitive incidents, counselors can gently ask for elaboration at critical points. All such emotional confrontations induced by therapists or counselors should be handled gently and with compassion.

Expressing Anger

Anger is bothersome for more than a few people. Many find it difficult to express because they never have learned how to use it effectively. Bereavement compounds their difficulties. Grievers are appalled to find themselves angry at the deceased or at God. Or they strike out against friends and family—the very people whom they most need for love and support.

It is important, therefore, that the therapist validate anger when it is justified, encouraging its expression in helpful ways. The bereaved need people who will not avoid, judge, or retaliate. Some clients may need to evaluate how they use anger in order to learn how it is disrupting social relationships and the peace that they so badly need.

Expressing Guilt

Switzer (1970) views guilt both as one of the several emotions that combine to produce the grief state, and as a complicating factor in grief. Either way, at the death of a significant person guilt anxiety almost inevitably is triggered. Glick et al. (1974) find guilt is expressed through: (a) subjective experience, (b) hostility, (c) self-punishing behavior, (d) self-justifying behavior, (e) compensatory behavior, and (f) attention-getting behavior. In their study about half the widows showed their guilt by talking about how they had tried to save their husbands and how they continue to suffer afterwards. The authors refer to this as "residual guilt."

Counselors must remember to differentiate between appropriate and inappropriate guilt. A husband who took a mistress and almost completely ignored his wife on her deathbed has an appropriate reason to feel guilty after she dies. However, the woman who for two years nursed her sick father but was not with him during the final moments should not feel guilty. Grief often amplifies guilt because "death has cut off opportunities for atonement, forgiveness, reconciliation" (Switzer, 1970, p. 134). Even when guilt is justified self-punishment has limited usefulness and endless self-recrimination is futile. The bereaved person may have to learn how to grant forgiveness to himself or herself. The counselor can help by offering restitution and understanding.

Apparent Absence of Feelings

Wortman and Silver (1989) maintain that not everyone experiencing a serious loss will necessarily show distress or depression; they cite studies—of widows, Mormon elderly, and those suffering spinal cord injuries—that find the majority of respondents did not show these symptoms. Other authorities would explain these apparent absences of reactions as temporary. Rosenblatt (1983) found from his study of diaries that the bereaved often think and act at times as though no loss has occurred—and appear to suffer no ill effects. Simos (1979) reminds us that many of the bereaved withdraw into themselves—some for respite between emotional episodes, others, instead of showing their feelings. Most authors see that some withdrawal is understandable in the face of the severe blow the bereaved have been dealt. But when withdrawal has become the dominant response, repression and some form of psychic numbing might be indicated. This latter phenomonon was described in chapter 2 as the diminished capacity to feel, a way of limiting experiences that are too threatening or too overwhelming to absorb or respond to in ordinary ways. Numbing also impairs the balance in a person's time relationships—the balance between past and future orientation (Lifton, 1982).

Counselors and therapists confronted by clients who show little or no feelings must recall the possibility that not everyone needs to ventilate emotions. However, if the clients came seeking assistance yet show few feelings after having experienced an obviously excruciating loss, action is called for. One way is to gently nudge them to again face the circumstances surrounding the loved one's death through a series of questions. Ask for details and how they feel about various events. If clients grow restless and irritated help them explore what lies behind those responses. Note if they struggle to remain aloof. Only the skilled clinician, however, should push beyond the point where the client displays defensiveness and anger.

REVIEWING DETAILS OF THE LOST RELATIONSHIP

It is essential that the bereaved review the circumstances surrounding the death and the history of the lost relationship. Grief work is, among other things, a re-examination with refeeling of much that is related to the death (Freese, 1977). If the griever has much to reconstruct in her or his life—emotionally, cognitively, and spiritually—and if the lost person played a large part in shaping past reality, these activities can be lengthy and emotional.

Most grievers, unless they are denying or avoiding reality, become preoccupied with and spend a great deal of time reviewing details of the lost relationship. This is important in helping them gain an understanding of what went on between them, what each sought from the other, and how the griever benefited and lost out as a consequence of the death. A useful question can be, What *don't* you miss about ———? "The way he always interrupted me when we were out places," one client said, "as if my opinion didn't really count for anything." That was the first negative comment she had made about her husband, and it led to a profitable analysis of how he had encouraged her to be herself in some ways but had squelched her in others.

In reviewing the history of lost relationships, clients frequently rediscover other losses, some from as far back as childhood. This provides an opportunity for the counselor to explore grieving styles. It is not uncommon to find that the predominant reaction to the first death in a person's life influences responses to all subsequent deaths. The author sometimes asks clients to select one adjective that characterizes their childhood reactions. These range from "terrified" and "overwhelmed" to "curious" and "delighted." One woman explained that the funeral for her grandfather when she was four years old was as much fun as any Christmas. While she found sadness from other deaths later on, she had difficulty understanding why some people so abhorred funerals.

One of the most bothersome tasks facing the griever and the therapist is resolving the many ambivalences or contradictions triggered by the loss. Ambivalence is the keynote to grief because of the intensity of feelings from conflicting impulses, the pain brought by awareness, and the difficulty of mastering those aroused feelings (Simos, 1979).

Historical reviews produce many unexpected results. Tournier (1984), for example, reports that while reflecting on his married life he would sense and become stimulated by his wife's living presence. Jacques (1973) writes about people rediscovering the fullness of life which, in turn, enhances loving feelings. Not just the central relationship being reviewed will be altered by changed perceptions; many relationships, present and past, can be reshaped. It is not uncommon to have widows discover new feelings about their fathers, for example, or for parents who lose a child to view their family obligations differently.

Reviews are important in one other way: To help the bereaved say goodbye to the deceased. Often the client will arrive at this conclusion, by himself or herself, perhaps by heaving a sigh at some point in the review and saying something like, "But that's all behind me now." Some will report on a singularly potent dream, so meaningful that it might be called a vision. In it the deceased indicates, often by words or actions, that it is time for the survivor to get on with his or her life. Sometimes it helps to have clients write a goodbye letter, either to leave at the grave site or to throw into the sea or a stream.

Histories can be difficult to control. Too many issues can pop up to be handled effectively during counseling sessions. They all might have relevance to where the client wants to emerge from the grief process, but your time together is limited. One way to work with a lengthening agenda is to help the client prioritize issues. The last session or two might be spent in discussing what he wishes to do about matters left undone or untouched. If continued counseling or therapy is not feasible or needed, it is important to help provide continued direction through referral to self-help groups or by suggesting individual activities. A relevant reading list can be provided or instructions given on how to keep a useful diary.

HELPING THE BEREAVED FIND THEIR OWN RESOURCES

An axiom for hospice personnel bears repeating for all professionals who help the bereaved: don't do it *for* them—help the bereaved find their own resources. Bowlby (1973) reminds us that people often are much more resourceful and stronger than we imagine. They grow to meet tragedies, especially if they are linked solidly with other humans who help them.

The way grievers perceive and use their support systems is a good barometer of their emotional state and social functioning. It is well to remember, however, that a support system consists of much more than friends and family. Osterweis et al. (1984) include the following:

- religious and other social rituals;
- values and beliefs by which individuals and families are comforted;

- shared norms that provide "meaning;"
- social networks that supply supportive needs;
- the availability and supply of nurturant others;
- the ability to seek and get support;
- the availability of supportive others who "permit" or elicit emotional release;
- structural supports such as community, work, and the like.

Osterweis et al. believe social supports enhance self-esteem and a feeling of being loved, help to solve problems, and provide relationship resources for meeting life cycle transitions. They warn, however, that "a support network that may be optimally helpful at one point in time may be dysfunctional at another time" (p. 203). It is generally believed among researchers, they conclude, that the characteristics of the social supports predict how well the person will cope with bereavement.

What kind of people do grievers find helpful? Obviously that differs from person to person and event to event, but from her research with widows, Raphael (1983) found three categories of helpers: those associated with the events preceding their husband's death; a new cast of helpers who appeared after the death; and the professionals in the management of death who overlapped both groups. She points out that the supportive community of mourners exists only briefly.

But what about people who appear not to need help, who are proud of their self-sufficiency? Bowlby (1973) points out that the self-reliant person usually is not so independent as cultural stereotypes make him out to be. One of the characteristics of the truly healthy griever is his or her ability to switch from independence to dependence and back again as the situation demands.

It is important for some of the bereaved to include sexual partners among their social network; sexual activity symbolizes for some people the renewal of life and an expression of a reconnection. Others lose all interest in sex, remaining celibate for long periods of time after the death of their spouses. Widowers appear more likely to retain sexual interest than widows (Glick, Weiss, & Parkes, 1974; Osterweis, et al., 1984).

Bereavement can be a time of sexual difficulties, however, rather than sexual promise. Freese (1977) discusses sexual problems the bereaved can encounter:

- withdrawal and a loss of interest in all the usual activities;
- impotency or frigidity;
- seeking sexual relations without tenderness and/or engaging in promiscuity;
- marrying out of sexual needs;

- in adolescent or preadolescent children, the hastening of sexual development.

WORKING WITH SPIRITUAL AND ·RELIGIOUS ISSUES

As stated elsewhere in this volume, the bereaved deserve and should expect assistance from the psychological practitioner in reworking their religious and spiritual beliefs. Foster (1986), herself a social worker, explains that the professional helper can do this in one of two ways:

- immerse herself or himself in understanding the particular belief system the client has adopted, e.g., specific religious creeds;
- explore individual variations, interpretations, and religious frameworks.

To do the latter, she warns, requires more than just a spiritual presence; the clinician must have knowledge and authentic understanding of religious matters.

Both of Foster's alternatives seem to require more preparation than busy professionals are able to put into any one case. How can a clinician hope to master a religious belief different from his or her own—a mainstream Protestant, for example, understanding Judaism? Determining a client's idiosyncratic set of beliefs seems even a greater impossibility. But it may not be so difficult or time consuming as it first appears.

How might you as a clinician go about this? Often it is less threatening to begin with spiritual rather than religious questions and to use an indirect approach. For example, if a client express the conviction that the deceased is better off dead, a follow-up question such as, "Where is the deceased now?" is one way of eliciting views on the life force as well as afterlife. A more direct approach would be to use one of the spiritual journey exercises described in chapter 6 or to ask for a spiritual autobiography.

Initiating discussions about a client's religious convictions can require more tact. To begin you need to identify and defuse whatever emotional reactions you have to his or her religious beliefs and spiritual expressions. Only then can the intellectual challenge of "cracking another's religious and spiritual code" be undertaken. These tasks involve (a) interpreting the other person's religious language, and (b) uncovering the deeper meanings of terms and concepts.

Interpreting another's religious language can be difficult. Landgraf (1987) explains that one's relationship to God can be explained only in special, personal language. It is necessary for the counselor to identify the concepts or images that the terms or phrases are describing. Take as an example this passage by Ohlrich (1983):

What . . . we seek in our despair, is an unveiling of God's heart, a vision of his face. Seeing God becomes the focus of our desire. In the midst of evil we want to find goodness in God, in the midst of ugliness we long for a vision of beauty in God, and by means of this discovery and this vision we want to transcend the evil and ugliness which engulfs us (p. 25).

"God's heart, a vision of his face" might be identified as, among other things, the goodness we seek for ourselves and the world. That passage might then be translated to read as follows:

What we seek in our despair, is a new unveiling of life's goodness and a vision of how that can be obtained. Remembering or recognizing examples of goodness makes me want to find other examples in my life. In the midst of the hate generated by my loss I want to find love; in the midst of the ugliness of my sorrow and pain, I long for the spiritual zest and beauty I knew as a child, and by means of this discovery and this vision, to transcend the tragedies that engulf me.

When a client talks of "sinning" clinicians might ask what has been violated. The "word of God" might be what a person holds most precious or sacred. Concepts of heaven could contain the ideals for someone's life, what she or he wishes for but doubts will ever materialize. The secret is not to accept the prima facie use of religious terms any more than one would of nonreligious terminology. Do not let overused God-talk or religious clichés obfuscate issues. Landgraf (1987) cites the case of a woman who refused to entertain any thought of leaving an abusive husband because she believed "loving is not an option for a Christian. It's Jesus' commandment" (p. 54).

When the discussion becomes murky counselors need to dig deeper for meanings. Take as one example references to the "supreme deity." Theologians themselves recognize that the concepts of "God," "Lord," and "The Father" are very abstract to many people (Ohlrich, 1983). A question to ask is, What does the belief in and loyalty to a deity represent? A client railing against God because "He took my wife" may feel betrayed because the "contract" he had worked out—I'll be a loyal worshiper; you, God, will protect me and my family—seems to have been violated. If this client viewed God as omniscient, omnipotent, and never changing, what does this imply for the rest of his life? Foster (1986) urges caregivers to listen with the "third ear" to the dynamic issues in people's lives such as unfulfilled hopes, shattered dreams, broken promises and sadnesses, sources of strength, and feelings of accomplishment and fulfillment.

Take as an example a woman client who raged against her Roman Catholic church. Her immediate justification for her anger was the failure of the local parish priest to arrive in time to administer last rites to her ailing mother. "My mother had been a loyal communicant for almost seventy years," she said. In response to questions it turned out that the priest did arrive, albeit too late. Because the client's anger appeared excessive, I asked her to sketch out her religious journey. Like her mother, she had conformed for many years to Roman Catholic practices and beliefs. But in her senior year of college she explored several religions, including the Society of American Friends. Her mother, who learned of this during her final illness, refused to understand or forgive. The client was able to connect her strong reaction to the priest's failure with her mother's attitude toward her religious experimentation. Eventually she learned that her anger was many-faceted—being closely tied to, among other things, the way she let family patterns keep her from exploring herself as a person.

Helping the client discover these obscure meanings can be risky; the therapist must be cautious (Kelsey, 1983). First, in order to discover new truths about the self and to find what makes life worth living, the seeker must confront her or his dark side, which can increase turmoil and despair. Furthermore, once certain truths about the self are glimpsed, action must be taken (Sinetar, 1986). Not to pursue these new visions leaves life meaningless. How often do all of us approach an insight only to realize, perhaps dimly in our unconscious, the frightening changes it will require in our lives. This increased sense of responsibility for ourselves and for others is one of the lessons Frankl (1978) learned at Auschwitz and Dachau. For him it became a "primordial anthropological fact that being human is being always directed, and pointing, to something or someone other than oneself: to a meaning to fulfill or another human being to encounter, a cause to serve or a person to love" (p. 35).

As people rise to new heights of understanding and challenge—heightened spirituality—they leave behind old patterns (Sinetar, 1986). Shuchter (1986) finds that from a deepening awareness of the fragility of life comes a keener appreciation of the beauty, richness, and importance of life. He also found among his subjects a "heightened empathic appreciation for the suffering of others," and "a more humanitarian view of the world" (p. 291).

However, these changes may not be fully within human power. Peck (1978) maintains that people reach these heights by allowing themselves to be propelled by a force "the mechanics of which we do not fully understand, that seems to operate routinely in most people to protect and to foster their mental health even under the most adverse conditions" (p. 238). This powerful force, which operates outside human consciousness, nurtures the spiritual growth of human beings. Most people describe this as God's love or power.

This section addresses complex, often controversial issues. Several authorities justifiably sound notes of caution. Fromm (1950) reminds us that "the analyst is not a theologian or a philosopher and does not claim competence in those fields" (p. 7). Robb (1986) warns psychologists against embracing supernaturalism. Kelsey (1983) observes that she is very cautious about taking clients too deeply into their spiritual lives. These warnings are much more applicable to therapists practicing in-depth, long-term therapies than to those using short-term counseling for the bereaved. Nevertheless, even within these time constraints, psychological practitioners have several important tasks to perform: affirming the importance of religious and spiritual concerns, helping clients identify principal issues, and pointing the way to continued spiritual and religious growth. The analyst, like the philosopher and theologian, must be concerned with the maintenance of the soul (Fromm, 1950).

Everyone needs ongoing guidance to continue with these tasks after the clinical relationship has terminated. If the client chooses not to affiliate with a religious organization, or seek out pastoral counseling, he or she might benefit from reading the Bible, the Talmud, the Koran, the writing of Zen masters, and other religious works. Clinicians should make a reading list available; it is most beneficial if they can discuss and recommend materials based on clients' expressed and perceived needs.

The bereaved's decision not to affiliate with a church or synagogue should be discussed. Religious growth is aided by a supportive religious community. It is this community that also provides the language necessary for the individual to "mediate among self, society, the natural world, and ultimate reality" (Bellah, Madsen, Sullivan, Swidler, & Tipton, 1985, p. 237). Clients may not be aware of the wide range of communities that exist, from the monolithic but relatively informal mainstream churches to the unbureaucratic but highly ritualistic Eastern religions. Clients can be helped by an explanation of the options. At that point a referral to a clerical leader of a church or pastoral counselor should be considered.

One final matter: What should a clinician do if the client asks him or her to join in praying together? If the counselor is accustomed to praying there should be little difficulty. Otherwise the counselor can suggest silent prayer and, if he or she does not wish to join, maintain a respectful silence.

The way a client prays can reveal much about the characteristics of her or his religious beliefs and level of faith. Is she or he subservient and largely helpless before an image of an all-powerful, unpredictable father? Or do the prayers reflect an underlying, joyous partnership with life? If prayer is a way of "giving oneself over to one's vision" (Fox, 1972, p. 124), shared prayers provide a glimpse into the client's vision and how he or she relates to and becomes involved in it. The client can be asked to discuss his or her method of prayer. With help, rote, meaningless exercises may be converted into moments of mystical renewal and expansion of awareness through a reflective dialogue with God or with that more hidden part of the self that reflects the most sacred part of all humanity.

The difficulties clinicians encounter when working with religious and spiritual matters decrease as the clients begin to recognize that the therapist will show respect in these matters. You may not please those who are looking for "one of their own faith." But if you show sincere interest in the attempts to deal with these broad issues there can form the partnership of the helper and the helped, (Pruyser, 1976, p. 83).

THE DIFFICULTY OF SEEMING TO DO TOO LITTLE

Those who work with the bereaved often feel at the end of the professional relationship that very little has been accomplished. This is not an uncommon reaction among mental health clinicians in general, but it may occur more frequently in grief work. Even when clients show deep and sincere appreciation, which, fortunately, happens often, we are left wondering how we have really helped them. Worden (1982) reminds us that there may be "something about the experience of grief which precludes [the therapist's] ability to help" (p. 107). It is useful to develop a mindset based on different definitions of success and competence. Doka (1986) suggested that clinicians learn to find satisfaction in small things; for example, when a deeply grieving person, following the client's suggestion to take long morning walks, begins to notice the beauties of early spring. Or when a widow decides to hang new curtains in her dining room as the first sign of renewed interest in her house. Sometimes the only reward is a slight spark of hope in a glance or a firm handshake of appreciation. But if we remain sensitive to the importance of these gestures, they can be profoundly gratifying.

Part III
Focus on the Counselor

Chapter 8

The Special Needs of the Professional

Lifton (1982) found that the people most effective with survivors of the holocaust, or with others who had experienced mass deaths, were those who had opened themselves up to the suffering and assumed it in some way, those who had become "survivors by proxy of that experience" (p. 226). The same can be said for any person who works with the bereaved. Kastenbaum (1987) refers to this experience as vicarious grief: the sorrow one feels with another. This emotion can lead to many close and empathic encounters that will leave their marks on us.

What kind of marks? We complete each encounter with a mixture of gratification for what we have learned and accomplished and of dissatisfaction and irritation for what was left undone. Over time one or the other of these reactions tends to predominate, leading either to discouragement and growing stress or to deep satisfaction. Stress and discouragement call for relief, satisfaction with our work can lead to further personal growth.

COUNTERACTING THE DISCOURAGEMENT

Beginning bereavement professionals believe they can handle these reactions to the working conditions without special attention and effort. The experienced know better. I shall begin by examining how the unpleasant results of bereavement work can be counteracted before turning my attention to how gratification from our labors can be increased.

Discouragement and growing stress from bereavement work can be counterbalanced by (a) proper self-maintenance, and (b) continual clarification of why one is engaged in bereavement work. Let us look at both of these points in more detail.

Proper Self-Maintenance

Empathy and compassion are precious but frail commodities that thrive under the favorable conditions of trust and loving concern but wither otherwise. The generic term used by the helping professions to enhance those favorable conditions is support.

As noted in chapter 7, support means far more than having someone to lean on or to listen to you—although most of us need both. Support comes from having our conscious thoughts and actions, and our more spontaneous reactions, affirmed by one or more respected "authorities." An authority can be our God, a learned scholar, a political figure, or a person accorded higher status within our family, social, or work group. An authority can be available in person, through his or her writings or recordings, or through the representations of others.

Person-to-person affirmation can be conveyed both verbally and nonverbally through facial and body expressions, touching, and voice tones. In addition to the informal expressions there are stylized and ritualistic ways of granting support as well, for example, through religious observances, the giving of awards, salary increases, and so on. Ironically, negative criticism, if presented in a way that enhances the worth of the individual, can be affirming; it delivers the message, "Even if I don't agree with what you did on this occasion, you are important enough to be helped."

Informal support is extended most often in situations where conversation between two or more people is spontaneous and relatively unstructured. Within the work place certain conditions foster these interactions: socially compatible colleagues, flexibility in the schedule, places for private meetings, and sympathetic supervisors. But more than informal support is necessary in high-stress work such as bereavement care. Raphael (1983) suggests that in those situations clinicians:

- share the burden of cases in supervisory sessions;
- find backup and relief for cases too difficult to bear;
- take officially-sanctioned breaks from such work.

Some organizations arrange more formal support activities. They provide regular group meetings, with or without outside therapists as leaders. Staff attendance usually is voluntary and the group itself controls the agenda. Other organizations try to alter their bureaucratic structure and control by encouraging staff to take time off to reduce stress and regain composure, reducing client load for those who are temporarily stressed, and rearranging schedules to permit staff to spend more or less time with clients as needed. These arrangements are easier to make when there are enough well-qualified staff, not a common condition in the health and human service fields. But if the administrators and supervisors want to support their clinical staff—and provide some support for themselves as well—they will find ways.

Staff support is not a luxury but a necessity. Without it clinicians in bereavement work can become dehumanized, causing them to distance themselves in relationships, experience fewer feelings, and become more mechanical and less caring in both their personal and professional lives. They can begin to exhibit psychosomatic symptoms, exhaustion, and much dissatisfaction with work and life in general; joy, good humor, and eagerness to tackle job assignments disappear. When these reactions occur intermittently, they usually can be managed; there is an almost endless array of useful stress-reduction techniques. When few or no changes occur, even after corrective steps have been taken, the professional faces burnout.

A person typically reacts to burnout in one of two ways, either by turning to less stress-producing work, or by crystalizing the dehumanizing defenses just described. Health and human service agencies lose many competent staff members as a consequence.

Clarification for Practicing Bereavement Work

Maintenance work will not be successful, however, if the practitioner does not remain clear about the reasons he or she has chosen to help those in grief. I have observed many professionals lose their early enthusiasm for hospice work within a few months; they resigned soon thereafter explaining that "hospices aren't for me." In exit interviews it became clear that their original expectations about working with the dying and bereaved were fuzzy at best. Many were not aware that their real motivations were to expiate guilt feelings from previous clinical or personal situations. Others had but a vague sense that hospice work would help them "mature," but the turmoil they encountered was too high a price to pay. I have observed that professionals who remain the longest with hospices, and who continue over the years to find personal as well as occupational satisfaction from their work, are those who best understand how they are serving their own as well as others' interests.

ENHANCING GRATIFICATION

Thousands of people work effectively for extraordinarily long days over lengthy periods of time, even in impossible situations. I do not refer to the most famous like Sister Teresa and Albert Schweitzer, but to those among us—nurses, physicians, the clergy, social workers, health aides, teachers, volunteers, and others—who persevere through great difficulties, able to find energy and mental resources for yet another task when others have given up from fatigue and frustration.

What is the source of this energy? Some claim it comes from healthy living, good diet, and regular exercise. This certainly helps, but there are physically unhealthy and impaired people who show the same kind of determination. I believe there is another source, what I choose to call *spiritual momentum.*

Importance of Spiritual Momentum

In chapter 4 we defined the spirit as the life force that moves people to seek out, nurture, and appreciate the good, the beautiful, and the truthful in life. Spiritual momentum keeps us pointed in those directions, overriding fatigue, discouragement, disappointments, defeats, and fear. The spirit stimulates one's talents to the fullest, resulting in creativity, ingenuity, and inspired problem-solving. The spirit also sensitizes awareness of one person to another, the condition Lifton (1982) found most useful for helping the bereaved.

How can the spirit be fostered? Quiet moments—what is referred to in this technological age as "down time"—are necessary to renew spiritual energy. These can be arranged in large blocks of time for retreats, or in shorter, more regular intervals through prayer, meditation, or noncompetitive physical activities such as jogging, biking, or swimming. Benson (1979) has studied how some joggers and hikers report reaching near-euphoric states that are similar to what is produced by prolonged, intensive meditation.

Prayer and meditation offer not only quiet time for spiritual renewal but encourage the flow of subconscious messages, what some refer to as God's voice, which direct one toward spiritual goals. These messages ordinarily get shut out by the press of everyday activities. Fox (1972, 1979) writes about how prayer and meditation can foster self-knowledge through creative inner dialogues. One need not retire to a sanctuary for this to happen; however, quiet times in a back yard or inside an automobile on long, unpressured drives may provide sufficient opportunity. Spiritual momentum can be impeded or encouraged by certain work conditions of which two appear to have especial relevance to bereavement work: using one's talents productively, and making nurturing connections.

Using Talents Productively

The spirit is fostered on the job to the degree that one uses his or her talents productively in service to a wider community. Energy for living surges when we produce a tangible object or a plan of action that has provided personal satisfaction and that others find useful and/or aesthetically appealing.

Only the individual knows when her or his talents are being used in ways that provide the most satisfaction. Schweitzer gave up worldwide recognition as a musician to build a medical center in the heart of Africa. I know a man who surrendered a promising career with the State Department to teach high school history. People often are willing to sacrifice a great deal to work at jobs of their choice. In the early years of the hospice movement many professionals left higher-salaried positions because serving the dying and the bereaved was their preferred occupation.

Not only does the clinician need to be enthusiastic about the labors to enhance spiritual momentum, he or she must become aware of how others are helped or aesthetically pleased by the efforts. The latter condition is not always possible to determine in bereavement care. As noted in chapter 7, grief is such an amorphous human condition, and clients typically are with counselors for such short periods of time, that it is difficult to determine changes in behavior and attitude. That is why forming nurturing human relationships is so important in our work.

Fostering Nurturing Connections

It is essential in bereavement care to foster human connections that nurture the professional as well as the person being served. The term "nurturing human connections" refers to those counselor–client transactions that increase each person's awareness of the other's humanness, meaning that the practitioner must expand the definition of the traditional clinical role. One anecdote may illustrate what is advocated.

While a member of a hospice staff, I was asked to help a family in which the elderly mother refused to accept the impending death of her adult daughter. Several previous conversations among family members and nurses had left the daughter's husband and the staff greatly disturbed. I accompanied the nurse to the family's house. We all sat for awhile around the patient's bed; she was nearly comatose. Then the mother and I went off to an adjoining room where she explained in great detail how her only daughter had overcome several childhood illnesses because of her "willpower;" she could do it again if she only tried harder and if we would offer more encouragement. It was a desperate litany. I heard her out, then asked for details about her three children and deceased husband.

It did not take long to discover common experiences between us, such as how we had worried about the effects of our spouses' death on the children. Neither of us, we confessed, did as well as we could have with them. She had, however, shown her caring in several admirable ways, and I told her so.

Later I said, "You loved your children very much."

"Yes," she replied quietly.

"And still do," I added.

She nodded.

In my mind I suddenly envisioned one of my adult children lying gravely ill in bed. After a pause I said, "I don't know how well I would hold up if one of my children were fighting cancer as yours is."

It took a while but she finally looked me straight in the eyes and asked softly, "My daughter's dying, isn't she?"

"Yes," I replied, startled by the sudden turn-around. After a few more words it was clear she needed to be alone, so I excused myself and left. In the car returning to the office, the nurse asked me what I had done to produce the change in her. I didn't know at first. Later that day I pondered the episode while alone. I was filled with extraordinary feelings, far stronger and deeper than mere gratification from a task well done. The mother and I had connected by mutually recognizing the tragedy of losing a child, a connection that meant she was no longer alone with her pain and fears. That realization enabled her, I am certain, to face the truth of her daughter's condition.

Many readers will have difficulty understanding "nurturing connections." Most of us are imbued with a different construct, the contractual relationship, which is an arrangement between two or more people based on maintaining a balance between what is given and what is received. The contractual basis for relationships permeates our society and is the prevalent assumption underlying most therapies (Bellah et al., 1985). The interactions in the above instance could be interpreted contractually: The mother was helped to face up to reality, and I, as counselor, was left with good feelings and a sense of accomplishment. But far more than that exchange actually occurred. We both were nurtured by a common, connecting experience, a concern for the other, that was not fed by balance or by measuring outcomes, one against the other. A nurturing connection is one of life's ironies, for it feeds personal satisfaction by diverting a person's attention away from personal needs.

Some will interpret what is being advocated as transference/countertransference or emotional bonding. Clearly emotions come into play. When I encountered the mother at the funeral two days later we clearly were drawn to one another. But nurturing connectiveness runs deeper than emotional bonding. Some might describe it as spiritual bonding—when two people sense a connection not only with each other but with a sense of transcendent beauty and wholesomeness. This explains why we feel so good at times when we help others selflessly.

Another way of explaining nurturing connections is provided by Cowan (1987) in his definition of love. For Cowan, love is "the capacity and commitment to let the emerging stories of others matter to us even as our own stories naturally matter" (p. 63). By taking in other people's "world of meaning," our own lives are made larger and enriched qualitatively. While connecting in nurturing ways both parties experience a transfer of meaning and understanding which, while possibly different in content, will share common references and be of mutual importance to both.

Hospice professionals form many nurturing connections. When I once asked survivors of clients to evaluate our services, their written and telephone messages were replete with comments about how wonderful and thoughtful individual members of the staff had been. Variations on the theme, "She became like a member of the family," were often heard. Even more revealing were (and are to this day) the ways survivors greet the staff with hugs, tender words, and misty eyes at the periodic memorial services held many weeks, for some, many months, after service has terminated.

It can be dangerous to encourage clients, who may be vulnerable from having lost an important relationship, to foster this kind of connection. Clinicians must be alert to signs that clients are misinterpreting their own and the counselor's feelings. There are important boundary lines that must be maintained. These are difficult to determine administratively (other than obvious restrictions about certain sexual and social behavior); each professional must determine for himself or herself—and must reassess each case based on what is learned about the individuals involved—the behavior and emotional commitment he or she is comfortable with. Some hospice nurses and social workers, for example, seldom give out their home phone numbers; others will do that, but will not meet the client anywhere but in the client's home or the hospice offices.

The difficulties and potential dangers of encouraging less formal relationships should not overshadow the importance of forming nurturing connections. The bereaved experience considerable separation, from the person or persons they lost, and from friends, family, and colleagues with whom they no longer can relate. Their grief has cast them adrift on a raft of isolation. Old friends do not comprehend their conflicting feelings and thoughts. Grievers embarrass others, and are embarrassed in turn, by their preoccupation, idleness, tears, and the desire to be alone.

Even when the bereaved begin to reconnect they encounter difficulties: The world has become a different place; their style of living has changed, as has the way they look at the world. They no longer value things that were of paramount importance a few months before—work, making money, taking care of a house, or keeping up with a busy social calendar. They may feel unusual, or different from former friends and some family. They wonder if, in their altered condition, they ever again can reconnect with people, the familiar, and their explanations of the unknown.

A professional cannot offer reassurance just with words and cannot instruct someone on how to reconnect with the world. Verbal messages

may at these times be the least effective medium. A griever is highly
sensitive to the reactions of others. Clinicians who remains distant and
aloof while advising clients on how to find nurturing provides further
evidence to the grievers that people are not willing to accept them as they
are.

How does one make a nurturing connection? There is no recipe. It
certainly cannot be contrived. Nurture arises from empathy and compassion for another person's condition. It is fostered by (a) a willingness to
allow another to sense one's feelings, attitudes, and images that are usually
kept in reserve; and (b) a heightened sensitivity to those attributes in the
other person. This allows both parties to be understood and their feeling
states to be sensed from a variety of verbal and non-verbal clues. A nurturing relationship can be recognized through a growing feeling of warmth
and an alertness to and focus on the other person. There usually is a mutual
pull, one toward the other, which manifests itself in subtle ways, such as
by standing and leaning closer together, or touching. Eye contact can be
intense and prolonged. While these responses resemble sexual attractiveness there is a more generalized euphoria rather than a concentration of
feelings in the sexual organs. There is much about a nurturing relationship
that resembles feelings of love, only in less intense ways.

Is connecting with clients in this way risky for the clinician? Is it healthy
to make even modest investments in relationships, even for a short time?
Why risk the possibility of adding to the unpleasant aspects of bereavement work by having to continually break off attachments to people you
have grown to like? These are fair questions. They reflect the concerns
many physicians and nurses struggle with when asked to provide more
humane care to dying patients—and why many of them follow the idiom
to "treat diseases, not people." They have not yet learned that each nurturing, spiritual transaction is sufficient unto itself, because the connection is
both with the individual and with a universal sense of humanness. The
feelings of loss that result from most leave-takings are offset by the en-
hanced awareness that what transpired between the two of you remains
unbroken regardless of distance, infrequency of future contacts, or even
total absence. A nurturing connection can bring both persons into contact
with the essence of human relationships, the central core experiences we
all seek from others. Once this is realized between people, even as a
minuscule glimmer, it cannot be lost. Therefore, close physical proximity
does not need to be prolonged, nor does the relationship necessarily need
to be converted into something more long-term or more emotionally-
intense. Disconnecting need not become a termination and can be done
naturally, without complications. Still, at times, it is difficult to say good-
bye.

Nurturing relationships can keep many clinicians working in situations that are otherwise intolerable. As one social worker told me, "I have to get away from the craziness of the office; it's the contacts with families that keeps me sane." Finding nurturance from human service produces more than "job satisfaction;" it will affect one's entire life. When professionals say "I've grown on this job," they are describing changes in their personal lives as well, whether or not they are immediately aware of it. The way we learn to interact with and show concern for clients influences the way we conduct our affairs at home and with friends. The opposite is just as true. We can say that professional and personal growth enhance one another and lead to a state of fulfillment. It is important to examine that process more carefully.

THE CHALLENGES OF FULFILLMENT

Growth in understanding and competence on the job usually inspires new visions and challenges. The career of one of our hospice nurses, Pat, illustrates that point. While in graduate school she signed on as a volunteer family caregiver, making known early her interest in future nursing openings. The dying have much to teach me, she explained. Employed by us a few months later, she served with distinction for over five years. She then resigned to become an independent, wholistic health practitioner, a "very risky" choice, she confessed. The decision to operate outside an agency was prompted in part by the need for greater freedom to offer her unique blend of nursing and spiritual care.

Pat's story is about personal fulfillment as well as professional competence; first when she chose to serve the dying and bereaved, again when she decided to move on to something different. Personal fulfillment is one of those conditions that is easily understood by those who have experienced it and virtually impossible to describe to people who have not. It includes a deep acceptance of self and satisfaction with what is accomplished. Fulfillment comes from expressing and receiving love, affection, and caring in a variety of forms from a variety of sources. It involves a balance, different for each person, between the mind and the soul, that is, among the emotions, the intellect, and the spirit. The state of fulfillment is fed by spiritual momentum.

Personal fulfillment becomes a solid platform and a secure foundation from which to engage in life's drama. A fulfilled person need not often waste energy or divert attention to ego-supporting activities. While experiencing fulfillment, one is able to reach out to others more easily, and to take risks that otherwise would be intolerable. The fulfilled person is able to look beyond the self and those emotionally close, to an ever enlarging sphere of people with whom he or she feels a kinship. Fulfillment projects one beyond immediate engagements, encouraging visions of what else might be accomplished, and how others in the world might benefit. These kinds of visions are scary. They undoubtedly mean that one must assume greater responsibilities for the self and for others. New responsibilities mean starting off on another quest, the possible loss of status, and the risk of failure. Many professionals cannot take those chances—at least not at first. Some of them, however, suddenly gain such abilities later in life.

The Need for Discipline and Determination

Counteracting the detrimental effects of bereavement care—through proper self-maintenance and the clarification of why one wishes to do grief counseling—and enhancing professional satisfaction in ways that can lead to personal fulfillment does not just happen. We all have to work at it to remain determined and to exercise discipline.

Peck (1978) describes discipline as "the basic set of tools we require to solve life's problems" (p. 15). The tools he refers to are: delay of gratification, acceptance of responsibility, dedication to truth, and balancing—the discipline that provides flexibility in life. Determination is the "stick-to-itiveness" that keeps people pointed toward a goal or desired image over a prolonged period of time in spite of difficulties and setbacks.

It is no easy matter to maintain spiritual discipline and determination outside a human group and/or an established body of thought and practice. To go it alone requires considerable study of extinct and existing religions and philosophies, great ingenuity, and considerable time. Even then there is a danger of failing to benefit from the accumulated wisdom and religious faith of the ages, and of falling victim to self-delusions. Religious communities help to foster similar values and systematically codified beliefs and faith statements. Rituals and other practices enhance beliefs. All these features encourage individuals to connect with some sense of the ultimate and everlasting reality.

Not all established religions are good places to experience the spiritual awakening that fosters personal development. The more authoritarian churches can paralyze the spirit by destroying spontaneity or can squelch individual imagination through forced conformity, thereby robbing both the ego and its soul of their right to grow. Churches vary greatly along an authoritarian dimension.

Many psychological practitioners, unable to accept the organized religions of their parents, have turned to humanism or the human potential movement as their "religion." This loosely-organized movement has some of the characteristics of all formal religions: it fosters the search for truth and goodness; brings like-minded people together for spiritual renewal;

thrives on a more-or-less common set of rituals and music; provides explanations of, and attempts to prepare people for, death; and finally, helps individuals become aware of and establish contact with an ultimate reality that includes a univeral, if not necessarily divine, presence.

Other psychologists have turned their backs on all forms of religion. However, Fromm (1950) maintains that everyone has a religious self; the issue is what kind of religion each will practice. Some of them have covertly tried to make a religion of science (Peck, 1978). Science, however, fails religiously on several counts, only one of which need be cited here—its inability to help individuals accommodate to their inevitable deaths. This forever unknowable event must be accounted for by one's faith. Death is the ultimate personal challenge, demanding explanations beyond what can be provided by scientific data—at least those that are presently available.

Whether or not formal Western religions, Eastern religions, humanism, or some other religious form is considered, it is up to the individual to select the practices and body of knowledge that would most help him or her maintain the discipline and effort needed to counterbalance the difficulties of human service. No one else—no group or institution—can make those decisions for a person.

As we grow in understanding of life, we increase opportunities to help others. As we help others, our own lives in turn become mysteriously richer, more complicated and difficult, but far more fulfilling and satisfying. It would be nice if fulfillment could be achieved with less effort, or in more simplistic ways. We all know the temptations: to live alone to avoid the turbulence of human relationships, to live without love to avoid the pain of loss, to hide within a group to avoid individual responsibility, to adopt simplistic explanations for human behavior and become dedicated to simplistic causes, to engage in routine work that creates few stresses. The greater the challenges the more vivid becomes the panoply of life.

Whatever the personal cost of our labor, those of us in bereavement care know it is well worth it. Bereavement work allows us to be drawn more fully into the richness and warmth of life as we glimpse how others struggle with all that is basic yet glorious in their lives. The bereaved, having faced the ending of a life they so dearly loved, examine in one way or another how they are living their own lives, and how they are relating to other people and to the eternal verities. The counselors, as partners to that process, may learn about aspects of human behavior and ways that professionals can connect to clients that may not be available to other clinicians. I believe bereavement counseling has a unique contribution to make to the human and health services—and beyond that, to the struggle of humankind to enhance what is good, beautiful, and honest in life itself. That may sound like an impossible dream—but one we all need.

Appendix A

Personal Grieving Style Inventory

Grief is a natural response to a felt loss, our way of repairing emotional damage. Each of us grieves differently from everyone else, and each time our grief is different than before. But a pattern forms, and becomes a person's grieving style.

The purpose of this worksheet is to help you, in a somewhat systematic way, reflect upon and better understand your own grieving style. To accomplish that goal it is important that you be honest with yourself, even if some of the memories are difficult and painful to recall.

Take your time; this worksheet is yours to keep. If it is not completed at the first sitting return to it later.

The information you provide on this worksheet is confidential; you will determine with whom, if anyone, it will be shared.

I. RESPONSES TO PAST LOSSES

Please complete the following sentences. In case you have not yet had a traumatic loss from death in your life, think of another major loss from divorce or separation, a broken romance, a relocation, etc.

A. The First Remembered Significant Loss

1. The first death (major loss) I experienced was that of my
   I was——years old.
2. When I heard of the death (loss) I was (e.g., at work, studying, awakened from a sleep)
3. I responded by (e.g., continuing what I had been doing, crying, swearing)

129

4. My predominant emotional tone for the next few days was
5. The other major change in my life that occurred just before or soon
   after my first experience of death (loss) was

B. The Most Recent Loss

1. The most recent death (loss) I experienced was
2. When I heard of the death (loss) I was
3. I responded by
4. My predominant emotional tone for the next few days was
5. The other major change in my life that occurred just before or soon
   after this death (loss) was
6. My reactions to this death (loss) compared to the first were similar in
   that
7. My reactions were different in that

C. How I Respond to Losses

Sit back for a moment, close your eyes, and try to recapture other losses
in your life. You may think of an incident from childhood when a favorite
toy was taken from you, or when you moved from one house to another.
Memories of teenage romance or the loss of a job may come to mind. Try
to remember as many losses as you can and as many details as possible.
Focus especially on the feelings that were evoked. Can you discern any
patterns to your reactions?

When you are ready, complete these unfinished sentences.

1. Usually when I first hear of a death (loss) or impending death (loss)
   I react by
2. After a while my initial reaction is replaced by feelings of
3. My predominant emotional reaction for the next few days is
4. Upon reflection, I would describe the way I grieve as

II. ATTITUDES TOWARD AND BELIEFS ABOUT GRIEF AND BEREAVEMENT

To help you identify your attitudes about grief, respond to the following questions by using the initials *A* (agree), *NS* (not sure), or *D* (disagree).

_____ Grieving becomes more difficult when people "give in" to their sorrow.
_____ Having many sympathetic people around tends to prolong grief.

_____ Grieving for more than one year becomes abnormal.

_____ Bereavement is an opportunity for people to mature as well as a time of suffering.

_____ Grief is as powerful as love in shaping attitudes and behavior.

_____ Grief left unexpressed goes underground to reappear later.

_____ People never fully recover from the damage of major losses.

_____ Some people do not need to grieve, even after a serious loss.

_____ People can make their grieving "better" or "worse" by the way they choose to live during bereavement.

_____ A person's grief is abnormal when she or he sees or hears the dead person.

_____ An adult's renewed interest in someone of the opposite sex is a sure sign that bereavement has abated.

_____ A mother's loss of a young child is the most difficult grief of all to experience.

_____ Religious beliefs profoundly affect the way bereavement is expressed.

_____ Children should be shielded as much as possible from the effects of a death.

_____ Children up to adolescent years grieve differently than do adults.

III. QUESTIONS ABOUT GRIEF

Please complete the following sentences. If you wish to share your responses with the [counselor, teacher, workshop leader], tear off this section and leave it with him or her.

A. What frightens me the most about grief is

B. The aspect of grief I am most uncertain (or most confused) about is

C. When it comes to the subject of grief, the opinion I have that most people disagree with is

D. On the subject of grief and bereavement, what I would like to know more about is

2

Appendix B
The Unfolding Tapestry of My Life

INSTRUCTIONS FOR THE RESPONDENT

Take a moment to look over the accompanying worksheet. After you have looked at the chart for a few minutes, turn back to this page for some explanations of the categories at the top of the worksheet.

1. Calendar Years from Birth. Starting at the left column of the worksheet, number down the column from the year of your birth to the present year. If there are a substantial number of years in your life, you may wish to number the columns in 2-year intervals.

2. Place—Geographic and Socioeconomic. Here you may record your sense of place in several different ways. It could be the physical place you lived in at different times in your life, including the geographic area where you lived, or it could be your sense of your position in society or in the community. Record your sense of place in whatever way seems most appropriate to you.

3. Key Relationships. These can be any types of relationships that you feel had a significant impact on your life at the time. The persons mentioned need not be living now, and you need not have known them personally. (That is, they could be persons who influenced you through your reading or hearing about them, etc.)

Note: "The Unfolding Tapestry of My Life" is reprinted from FAITH DEVELOPMENT AND PASTORAL CARE by James W. Fowler, copyright © 1987 Fortress Press. Used by permission of Augsberg Fortress.

4. Uses and Directions of the Self. Here you can record not only how you spent your time but also what you thought you were doing at that time.

5. Marker Events. Here you may record the events that you remember which marked turning points in your life—moves, marriages, divorces, etc. Major events occur, and things are never the same again.

6. Age by Year. This column simply gives you another chronological point of reference. Fill it in with the same intervals you used for calendar years on the left-hand side of the chart.

7. Events and Conditions in Society. In this column we ask you to record what you remember of what was going on in the world at various times in your life. Record this as an image or phrase, or a series of images and phrases, that best sums up the period for you.

8. Images of God. This is an invitation for you to record briefly, in a phrase or two, what your thoughts or images of God—positive and negative— were at different times of your life. If you had no image of God or cannot remember one, answer appropriately.

9. Centers of Value and Power. What persons, objects, institutions, or goals formed a center for your life at this time? What attracted you, what repelled you, what did you commit your time and energy to, and what did you choose to avoid? Record only the one or two most important ones.

10. Authorities. This column asks to whom or what you looked to for guidance or to ratify your decisions and choices at various points in your life.

As you work on the chart, make brief notes to yourself indicating the thoughts you have under each of the columns. It is not necessary to fill out the columns in great detail. You are doing the exercise for yourself, so use shorthand or brief notes.

After you have finished your work with the chart, spend some time thinking about your life as a whole. Try to feel its movement and its flow, its continuities and discontinuities. As you look at the tapestry, let yourself imagine your life as a drama or a play. Where would the divisions of it naturally fall? If you were to divide it into chapters or episodes, how would these be titled? When you have a sense of how your life might be divided, draw lines through these areas on the chart and jot down the titles on the reverse side of the work sheet.

This is the unfolding tapestry of your life at this particular time. In the coming days or months you may want to return to it for further reflection or to add things that may come to you later. Some people find that the tapestry exercise is a good beginning for keeping a regular journal or diary. You may find, too, that if you come back to this exercise after some time has passed, the chapters and titles in your life will be different as you look at them in the light of new experiences.

Worksheet: The Unfolding Tapestry of My Life

Calendar Years From Birth	Place— Geographic and Socioeconomic	Key Relationships	Uses and Directions of the Self	Marker Events

Worksheet: The Unfolding Tapestry of My Life (*Continued*)

Age by Year	Events and Conditions in Society	Images of God	Centers of Value and Power	Authorities

References

Agosta, L. (1984). Empathy and intersubjectivity. In J. Lichtenberg, M. Bornstein, & S. Silver (Eds.), *Empathy* (pp. 43–61). Hillsdale, NJ: Lawrence Erlbaum Associates.

American Psychiatric Association. (1987). *Diagnostic and statistical manual of mental disorders* (3rd ed. rev.). Washington, DC: Author.

Arkin, A. (1981). Emotional care of the bereaved. In O. Margolis, H. Raether, A. Kutscher, J. Powers, I. Seeland, R. DeBellis, & D. Cherico (Eds.), *Acute grief: Counseling the bereaved* (pp. 40–44). New York: Columbia University Press.

Becker, E. (1973). *Denial of death.* New York: Free Press.

Bellah, R. N., Madsen, R., Sullivan, W. M., Swidler, A., & Tipton, S. M. (1985). *Habits of the heart: Individualism and commitment in American life.* New York: Harper & Row.

Benson, H. (1979). *The mind/body effect: How behavioral medicine can show you the way to better health.* New York: Simon & Schuster.

Bergin, A. E. (1983). Religiosity and mental health: A critical reevaluation and meta-analysis. *Professional Psychology, 14,* 170–184.

Bowen, M. (1976). Theory in the practice of psychotherapy. In P. J. Guerin, Jr. (Ed.), *Family therapy* (pp. 42–90). New York: Gardner Press.

Bowlby, J. (1969). *Attachment and Loss: Vol. I. Attachment.* New York: Basic Books.

Bowlby, J. (1973). *Attachment and Loss: Vol. II. Separation.* New York: Basic Books.

Bowlby, J. (1980). *Attachment and Loss: Vol. III. Loss, sadness and depression.* New York: Basic Books.

Brown, J. T. & Stoudemier, G. A. (1983). Normal and pathological grief. *Journal of the American Medical Association, 250,* 378–382.

Campbell, J. (1988). *An open life.* New Dimensions Foundation. Burdett, NY: Larson Publications.

Caroff, P. & Dobrof, R. (1975). The helping process and bereaved families. In B. Schoenberg, I. Gerber, A. Wiener, A. Kutscher, D. Perez, & A. Carr (Eds.), *Bereavement, Its psychosocial aspects* (pp. 232–242). New York: Columbia University Press.

Carse, J. P. (1981). Grief as a cosmic crisis. In O. Margolis, H. Raether, A. Kutscher, J. Powers, I. Seeland, R. DeBellis, & D. Cherico (Eds.). *Acute grief: Counseling the bereaved.* New York: Columbia University Press.

Clayton, P. J., Desmarais, L., & Winokur, G. (1968). A study of normal bereavement. *American Journal of Psychiatry, 125,* 168–174.

Corless, I. B. (1986). Spiritually for whom? In F. Wald (Ed.), *In quest of the spiritual component of care for the terminally ill: Proceedings of a colloquium* (pp. 85–96) Branford, CT: Yale University School of Nursing.

Cowan, M. A. (1987). Emerging in love: Everyday acts in ultimate contexts. In P. Pruyser (Ed.), *Changing views of the human condition.* Macon, GA: Mercer University Press.

Das, S. S. (1971). Grief and the imminent threat of non-being. *British Journal of Psychiatry, 118,* 467–68.

Demi, A. S. & Miles, M. S. (1987). Parameters of normal grief. *Death Studies, 11,* 397–412.

Doka, K. J. (1986). *Disenfranchised grief.* Paper presented at the Annual Meeting of the New York State Hospice Association, The Forum for Death Education and Counseling, College of New Rochelle, New Rochelle, NY.

Doka, K. J. & Jendreski, M. (1986). Spiritual support for the suffering: Clergy attitudes toward bereavement. *Loss, Grief, and Care, 1*(1–2), 155–160.

Dombeck, M. & Karl, J. (1987). Spiritual issues in mental health care. *Journal of Religion and Health, 26*(3), 183–197.

Ellerhorst-Ryan, J. (1985). Selecting an instrument to measure spiritual distress. *Oncology Nursing Forum, 12* (2), 93–99.

Engel, G. L. (1966). Is grief a disease? *Psychosomatic Medicine, 23,* 18–22.

Farberow, N. L., Gallagher, D. E., Gilenski, M. J., & Thompson, L. W. (1987). An examination of the early impact of bereavement on psychological distress in survivors of suicide. *Gerontologist, 27*(5), 592–598.

Ferguson, M. (1980). *The aquarian conspiracy.* Los Angeles: J. P. Tarcher.

Ferguson, T., Schorer, C. E., Tourney, G. & Ferguson, J. (1981). Bereavement, stress, and rescaling therapy. In O. Margolis, H. Rather, A. Kutscher, J. Powers, I. Seeland, R. DeBellis, & D. Cherico (Eds.), *Acute Grief: Counseling the bereaved* (pp. 158–166). New York: Columbia University Press.

Foster, R. J. (1978). *Celebration of discipline.* San Francisco: Harper & Row.

Foster, Z. (1986). Humanism as a foundation for spirituality: Its contribution to patients, families, caregivers and institutions. In F. Wald (Ed.), *In quest of the spiritual component of care for the terminally ill: Proceedings of a colloquium* (pp. 99–106). Branford, CT: Yale University School of Nursing.

Fowler, J. W. (1981). *Stages of faith.* San Francisco: Harper & Row.

Fowler, J. W. (1987). *Faith development and pastoral care.* Philadelphia: Fortress Press.

Fox, M. (1972). *On becoming a musical mystical bear.* New York: Paulist Press.

Fox, M. (1979). *A spirituality named compassion and the global village, humpty dumpty and us.* Minneapolis, MN: Winston Press.

Frankl, V. E. (1975). *The unconscious god.* New York: Simon & Schuster.

Frankl, V. E. (1978). *The unheard cry for meaning.* New York: Simon & Schuster.

Frederick, J. F. (1985). Possible failure of immunosurveillance system: Grief and cancer. In O. Margolis, H. Raether, A. Kutscher, S. Klagsbrun, E. Marcus, V. Pine, & D. Cherico (Eds.), *Loss, grief, and bereavement: A guide for counseling* (pp. 55–61). New York: Praeger.

Freese, A. (1977). *Help for your grief.* New York: Schocken Books.

Freud, S. (1961). The future of an illusion. In S. Freud, *The standard edition of the complete works of Sigmund Freud* (pp. 5–56). London: The Hogarth Press.

Freud, S. (1964). *Psychoanalysis and faith: The letters of Sigmund Freud and Oskar Pfister.* New York: Basic Books.

Fromm, E. (1950). *Psychoanalysis and religion.* New York: Bantam Books.

Fulmer, R. H. (1987). Special problems of mourning in low-income, single-parent families. *Family Therapy Collections, 23,* 19–37.

Glick, I. O., Weiss, R., & Parkes, C. M. (1974). *The first year of bereavement.* New York: John Wiley & Sons.

Glock, C. Y. (1962). On the study of religious commitment. *Religious Education, 57,* 598–610.

Goldstein, A. P. & Michaels, G. Y. (1985). *Empathy: Development, training and consequences.* Hillsdale, NJ: Lawrence Erlbaum Associates.

Gowin, D. B. (1981). *Educating.* Ithaca, NY: Cornell University Press.

Gramlich, E. P. (1968). Recognition and management of grief in elderly patients. *Geriatrics, 23*(7), 87–92.

Gustafson, J. P. (1986). *The complex secret of brief psychotherapy.* New York: W. W. Norton.

Harper, R. (1968). *The path of darkness.* Cleveland, OH: The Press of Case Western Reserve University.

Hillman, J. (1975). *Re-visioning psychology.* New York: Harper & Row.

Horowitz, M. J., Marmar, C., Krupnick, J., Wilner, N., Kaltreider, N., & Wallerstein, R. (1984). *Personality, styles and brief psychotherapy.* New York: Basic Books.

Jacobs, S. & Ostfeld, A. (1980). The clinical management of grief. *Journal of the American Geriataric Society, 28,* 331–335.

Jaques, E. (1973). Death and the mid-crisis. In H. M. Ruitenbeck (Ed.), *The interpretation of death.* New York: J. Aronson.

James, W. (1960). *The varieties of religious experience.* Glasgow: William Collins Sons. Co.

Jung, C. G. (1957). *The undiscovered self.* New York: New American Library.

Jung, C. G. (1960). *The structure and dynamics of the psyche.* New York: Pantheon Books.

Kalish, R., & Reynolds, D. (1981). *Death and ethnicity.* Farmingdale, NY: Baywood.

Kastenbaum, R. J. & Aisenberg, R. (1972). *The psychology of death.* New York: Springer Publishing Co., Inc.

Kastenbaum, R. J. (1987). Vicarious grief: An intergenerational phenomenon? *Death Studies, 11*(6), 447–453.

Kelly, G. A. (1963). *Theory of personality: The psychology of personal constructs.* New York: W. W. Norton.

Kelsey, M. T. (1983). *Transcend: A guide to the spiritual quest.* New York: Crossroad.

Kessler, B. G. (1987). Bereavement and personal growth. *Journal of Humanistic Psychology, 27,* 228–247.

Kleber, R. J. & Brom, D. (1985). Psychotherapy and pathological grief controlled outcome study. *Israel Journal of Psychiatry and Related Sciences, 24(1–2),* 99–109.

Kohut, H. (1984). Introspection, empathy, and the semicircle of mental health. In J. Lichtenberg, M. Bornstein, & D. Silver (Eds.), *Empathy* (pp. 81–100). Hillsdale, NJ: Lawrence Erlbaum Associates.

Krishnamurti, J. (1980). *Explorations into insight.* San Francisco: Harper & Row.

Kroll, J. & Sheehan, W. (1989). Religious beliefs and practices among 52 psychiatric inpatients in Minnesota. *American Journal of Psychiatry, 146*(1), 67–72.

Kubler-Ross, E. (1969). *On death and dying.* New York: Macmillan.

Kuhn, T. (1962). *The structure of scientific revolutions.* Chicago: University of Chicago Press.

Landgarten, H. B. (1981). *Clinical art therapy.* New York: Brunner Mazel.

Landgraf, P. A. (1987). Dealing with the religious client in pastoral counseling. *Journal of Pastoral Psychotherapy, 1*(2), 51–59.

Larson, D. B., Pattison, E., Blazer, D., Omran, A., & Kaplan, B. (1986). Systematic analysis of research on religious variables in four major psychiatric journals, 1978–1982, *American Journal of Psychiatry, 143,* 329–334.

Levinson, D. J., Darrow, C., Klein, E., Levinson, M., & McKee, B. (1978). *The seasons of a man's life.* New York: Ballantine Books

Lewis, C. S. (1961). *A grief observed.* Toronto: Bantam Books.

Lieberman, S. (1978). Nineteen cases of morbid grief. *British Journal of Psychiatry, 132,* 159–63.

Lifton, R. J. (1979). *The broken connection: On death and the continuity of life.* New York: Simon & Schuster.

Lifton, R. J. (1982). Apathy and numbing—a modern temptation. In F. Dougherty (Ed.), *The meaning of human suffering.* New York: Human Sciences Press.

Lindemann, E. (1944). Symptomatology and management of acute grief. *American Journal of Psychiatry 101,* 141–148.

MacLean, A. (1988). *The wind in both ears.* Boston: Unitarian Universalist Association.

Margolis, O. (1985). *Loss, grief, and bereavement: A guide for counseling.* New York: Praeger.

Marmar, C. R., Horowitz, M. J., Weiss, D. S., & Wilner, N. R. (1988). A controlled trial of brief psychotherapy and mutual-help group treatment of conjugal bereavement. *American Journal of Psychiatry, 145*(2), 203–209.

Marris, P. (1974). *Loss and change.* New York: Pantheon Book.

Maslow, A. (1971). *The farther reaches of human nature.* New York: Viking Press.

Mawson, D., Marks, I., Ramm, L., & Stern, R. (1981). Guided mourning for morbid grief: A controlled study. *British Journal of Psychiatry, 138,* 185–193.

May, R. (1980). Value conflicts and anxiety. In I. Kutash, L. B. Schlesinger and Associates (Eds.), *Handbook on stress and anxiety* (pp. 241–248). San Francisco: Jossey-Bass.

McCollough, C. R. (1983). *Heads of heaven, feet of clay: Ideas and stories for adult faith education.* New York: The Pilgrim Press.

McGill, A. (1982). Human suffering and the passion of Christ. In F. Dougherty (Ed.), *The meaning of human suffering.* New York: Human Sciences Press.

McGoldrick, M., Hines, L. P., & Preston, N. G. (1986). Mourning rituals. *Family Therapy Networker, 10*(6), 28–36.

McNiff, S. (1989). *Depth psychology of art.* Springfield, IL: Charles C. Thomas.

Melges, F. & DeMaso, D. R. (1980). Grief resolution therapy: Reliving, revising, and revisiting. *American Journal of Psychotherapy, 34*(1), 51–60.

Middleton, W. & Raphael, B. (1987) Bereavement: State of the art and science. *Psychiatric Clinics of North America, 10*(3), 329–343.

Moberg, D. O. (1984). Subjective measures of spiritual well-being. *Review of Religious Research, 25*(4), 351–364.

Ochs, C. (1983). *Women and spirituality.* Totowa, NJ: Rowman & Allanheld.

Ohlrich, C. (1983). *The suffering god: Hope and comfort for those who are hurt.* London: SP CK/Triangle.

Olinick, S. L. (1984). A critique of empathy and sympathy. In J. Lichtenberg, M. Bornstein & D. Silver (Eds.), *Empathy* (pp. 33–166). Hillsdale, NJ: Lawrence Erlbaum Associates.

Osterweis, M., Solomon, F., & Green, M. (Eds). (1984). *Bereavement: Reactions, consequences, and care.* Washington, DC: National Academy Press.

Parkes, C. M. (1980). Bereavement counseling: Does it work? *British Medical Journal, 281,* 3–6.

Parkes, C. M. (1981). Psychosocial care of the family after the patient's death. In O. Margolis, H. Raether, A. Kutscher, J. Powers, I. Seeland, R. DeBellis, & S. Clerico (Eds.), *Acute grief: Counseling the bereaved* (pp. 53–68). New York: Columbia University Press.

Parkes, C. M. (1987–1988). Research: Bereavement. *Omega 18*(4), 365–377.

Parkes, C. M. & Weiss, R. (1983). *Recovery from bereavement.* New York: Basic Books.

Peach, M. R. & Klass, D. (1987). Special issues in the grief of parents of murdered children. *Death Studies, 11*(2), 81–88.

Peck, M. S. (1978). *The road less traveled.* New York: A Touchstone Book, Simon & Schuster.

Pelletier, K. R. & Garfield, C. (1976). *Consciousness: East and west.* New York: Harper Colophon Books.

Pelletier, K. (1978). *Toward a science of consciousness.* New York: Delacorte.

Pollock, G. H. (1987). The mourning–liberation process in health and disease. *Psychiatric Clinics of North America 10*(3), 345–355.

Proudfoot, W. (1985). *Religious experience.* Berkeley: University of California Press.

Proulx, J. R. & Baker, P. D. (1981). Grief, grieving, and bereavement: A look at the basics. In O. Margolis, H. Raether, A. Kutscher, J. Powers, I. Seeland, R. DeBellis, & J. Cherico (Eds.), *Acute grief: Counseling the bereaved* (pp. 191–198). New York: Columbia University Press.

Pruyser, P. W. (1976). *The minister as diagnostician.* Philadelphia: The Westminister Press.

Purisman, R. & Maoz, B. (1977). Adjustment and war bereavement: Some considerations. *British Journal of Medical Psychology, 50*(1), 1–9.

Raphael, B. (1977). Preventive intervention with the recently bereaved. *Archives of General Psychiatry, 34,* 1450–1454.

Raphael, B. (1980). A psychiatric model for bereavement counseling. In B. M. Schoenberg (Ed.), *Bereavement counseling: A multidisciplinary handbook* (pp. 147–172). Westport, CT: Greenwood Press.

Raphael, B. (1983). *The anatomy of bereavement.* New York: Harper & Row/Basic Books.

Raphael, B., & Middleton, W. (1987). Current state of research in the field of bereavement. *Israel Journal of Psychiatry and Related Sciences,* 24(1–2), 5–32.

Reed, G. S. (1984). The antithetical meaning of the term "empathy" in psychoanalytical discourse. In J. Lichtenberg, M. Bornstein, & D. Silver (Eds.), *Empathy* (pp. 7–24). Hillsdale, NJ: Lawrence Erlbaum Associates.

Rees, W. D. (1971). The hallucinations of widowhood. *British Medical Journal, 4,* 37–41.

Robb, H. B. (1986). Symposium: Spiritual issues—do they belong in psychological practice? Introduction. *Psychotherapy in Private Practice, 4*(4), 85–91.

Rosenblatt, P. C. (1983). *Bitter, bitter tears.* Minneapolis: University of Minneapolis Press.

Rynearson, E. K. (1987). Psychotherapy of pathological grief. *Psychiatric Clinics of North America, 10*(3), 487–499.

Schneider, J. (1984). *Stress, loss and grief.* Rockville, MD: Aspen Systems Corporation.

Schneider, J. (1989, Autumn). The transformative power of grief. *Noetic Sciences Review,* 26–31.

Schön, D. A. (1983). *The reflective practitioner: How professionals think in action.* New York: Basic Books.

Shapiro, T. (1984). Empathy: A critical reevaluation. In J. Lichtenberg, M. Bornstein, & D. Silver, *Empathy* (pp. 103–128). Hillsdale, NJ: Lawrence Erlbaum Associates.

Sheehy, G. (1974). *Passages.* New York: E. P. Dutton.

Shuchter, S. R. (1986). *Dimensions of grief: Adjusting to the death of a spouse.* San Francisco: Jossey Bass.

Silverman, P. R. & Silverman, S. M. (1975). Withdrawal in bereaved children. In B. Schoenberg, I. Gerber, A. Wiener, A. Kutscher, A. Peretz, D. Peretz, & A. Carr (Eds.), *Bereavement, its psychosocial aspects* (pp. 208–214). New York: Columbia University Press.

Silverman, P. R. (1981). *Helping women cope with grief.* Beverly Hills: Sage Publications.

Simos, B. G. (1979). *A time to grieve.* New York: Family Service Association of America.

Sinetar, M. (1986). *Ordinary people as monks and mystics.* New York: Paulist Press.

Singh, K. (1959). Spirituality, what is it? *Shakti Nagar,* Delhi, India: D. V. Sharma.

Smith, C. R. (1982). *Social work with the dying and bereaved.* London: Macmillan Press.

Spilka, B. (1986). Spiritual issues: Do they belong in psychological practice? Yes—but! *Psychotherapy in Private Practice, 4*(4), 93–100.

Stokes, K. (1987). *Faith development in the adult life cycle: The report of a research project.* Minneapolis: Religious Education Associates.

Stokes, K. (1989). *Faith is a verb.* Mystic, CT: Twenty-third Publications.

Stoll, R. (1979). Guidelines for spiritual assessment. *American Journal of Nursing, 79*(9), 1574–1577.

Stroebe, W., & Stroebe, M. S. (1987). *Bereavement and health: The psychological and physical consequences of partner loss.* New York: Cambridge University Press.

Switzer, D. (1970). *The dynamics of grief.* Nashville, TN: Abingdon Press.

Tillich, P. (1957). *Dynamics of faith.* New York: Harper Torchbooks.

Tournier, P. (1984). The blessings of a deep loss. *Christianity Today, 25*(17), 28–29.

Vachon, M. L. S., Sheldon, A., Lancee, W., Lyall, W., Rogers, J., & Freeman, S. (1982). Correlates of enduring stress patterns following bereavement: Social network, life situation, and personality. *Psychological Medicine, 12,* 783–788.

Veroff, J., Kulka, R. A., & Douvan, E. (1981). *Mental health in America: Patterns of help-seeking from 1957 to 1976.* New York: Basic Books.

Volkan, V. D. (1975). Regrief therapy. In B. Schoenberg, I. Gerber, A. Wiener, A. Kutscher, D. Peretz, & A. Carr (Eds.), *Bereavement, its psychological aspects* (pp. 334–350). New York: Columbia University Press.

Worden, J. W. (1982). *Grief counseling and grief therapy: A handbook for the mental health practitioner.* New York: Springer.

Wortman, W. B. & Silver, R. C. (1989). The myths of coping with loss. *Journal of Consulting and Clinical Psychology, 57*(3), 349–357.

Zisook, S., Devaul, R. A., & Click, M. A. (1982). Measuring symptoms of grief and bereavement. *American Journal of Psychiatry, 139,* 1590–1593.

Bibliography

Aberbach, D. (1987). Grief and mysticism. *International Review of Psycho-Analysis, 14,* 509–526.

Baier, K. (1987). The purpose of man's existence. In O. Hanfling (Ed.), *Life and Meaning: A reader* (pp. 20–33). New York: Basil Blackwell.

Berger, P. L. (1969). *The sacred canopy: Elements of a sociological theory of religion.* Garden City, NY: Anchor Books.

Bowlby, J. (1962). Pathological mourning and childhood mourning. *Journal of the American Psychoanalytical Association, II,* 500–541.

Bowlby, J. (1977). The making and breaking of affectional bonds. *British Journal of Psychiatry, 130,* 421–431.

Breton, S. (1982). Human suffering and transcendence. In F. Dougherty (Ed.), *The meaning of human suffering.* New York: Human Sciences Press.

Bugen, L. A. (1977). Human grief: A model for prediction and intervention. *American Journal of Orthopsychiatry, 47,* 196–206.

Buxton, M. E., Smith, D. E., & Seymour, R. B. (1987). Spirituality amd the other points of resistance to the 12-step recovery process. *Journal of Psycho-Active Drugs, 19*(3), 275–286.

Calabrese, J. R., Kling, M. A., & Gold, P. W. (1987). Alterations in immunocompetence during stress, bereavement, and depression: Focus on neuroendocrine regulation. *American Journal of Psychiatry, 144*(9), 1123–1134.

Chittister, J. D. & Marty, M. E. (1983). *Faith & ferment.* Minneapolis: Augsburg.

Clayton, P. J., (1982) Bereavement. In E. S. Paykel (Ed.), *Handbook of affective disorders.* London: Churchill Livingstone.

Collins, W. E. (1987). Keeping the therapist alive. *Journal of Religion and Health, 26*(3), 206–213.

Deutsch, D. (1982). *The development, reliability and validity of an instrument designed to measure grief.* Unpublished doctoral dissertation, Michigan State University, East Lansing, MI.

DeVaul, R. A. (1975). Clinical aspects of grief and bereavement. *Primary Care, 6*(2), 391–402.

Dore, C. (1984). Does suffering serve valuable ends? *Philosophy and Phenomenological Research, 45,* 103–110.

Elbirlik, K. (1983). The mourning process in group therapy. *International Journal of Group Psychotherapy, 33*(2), 215–227.

Erickson, R. C. (1987). Spirituality and depth psychology. *Journal of Religion and Health, 26*(3), 198–205.

Finkelstein, H. (1988). The long-term effects of early parent death. *Journal of Clinical Psychology, 44*(1), 3–9.

Frankl, V. E. (1963). *Man's search for meaning.* New York: Pocket Books.

Gauthier, J. & Pye, C. (1979). Graduated self-exposure in the management of grief. *Behaviour Analysis and Modification, 3,* 202–208.

Geller, J. (1985). The long-term outcome of unresolved grief: An example. *Psychiatric Quarterly, 57*(2), 142–146.

Graves, J. S. (1978). Differentiating grief, mourning, and bereavement. *American Journal of Psychiatry, 135,* 874–875.

Gould, R. L. (1978). *Transformations: Growth and change in adult life.* New York: Simon & Schuster.

Halmos, P. (1978). *The faith of the counselors.* London: Constable.

Hanfling, O. (1987). *Life and meaning.* Cambridge, MA: Basil Blackwell.

Hillman, J. (1967). *Insearch: Psychology and religion.* Dallas, TX: Spring Publications.

Hogan, R. A. & Lienhart, G. A. (1985). The preparation of a crisis counselor for the terminally ill and their families. In O. Margolis, H. Raether, A. Kutscher, S. Klagsbrun, E. Marcus, V. Pine, & D. Cherico (Eds.) *Loss, grief, and bereavement: A guide for counseling* (pp. 108–116). New York: Praeger.

Hoxeng, D. D. (1980). Fear of death and its implications for death milieu counseling. In B. Schoenberg, (Ed.), *Bereavement counseling: A multidisciplinary handbook.* Westport, CT: Greenwood Press.

Hyer, L., Jacob, M. R., & Patison, E. M. (1987). Later-life struggles: Psychological/spiritual convergence. *Journal of Pastoral Care, 41*(2), 141–149.

Irwin, M., Daniels, M., Risch, S. C., Bloom, E., & Weiner, H. (1988). Plasma cortisol and natural killer cell activity during bereavement. *Biological Psychiatry, 24,* 173–178.

Jacobs, S. C., Nelson, J. & Zisook, S. (1987). Treating depressions of bereavement with antidepressants: A pilot study. *Psychiatric Clinics of North America, 10*(3), 501–510.

Jacobs S. C., Mason, J., Kosten, T.R., & Ksal, S.V., (1987). Urinary free cortiso and separation anxiety early in the course of bereavement and threatened loss. *Biological Psychiatry, 22*(2), 148–152.

Jaffe, D. T. (1985). Self-renewal: Personal transformation following extreme trauma. *Journal of Humanistic Psychology, 25*(4), 99–124.

James, J. W. & Cherry, F. (1988). *The grief recovery handbook: A step-by-step program for moving beyond loss.* New York: Harper Row.

Jerrigan, H. L. (1976). Bringing together psychology and theology: Reflections of ministry to the bereaved. *Journal of Pastoral Care, 30*(2), 88–102.

Jung, C. G. (1964). *Civilization in transition.* Princeton, NJ: Princeton University Press.

Karl, G. T. (1987). A new look at grief. *Journal of Advanced Nursing, 12*(5), 641–645.

Kelsey, M. T. (1984). *Christopsychology.* New York: Crossroad.

Knott, J. E., Ribar, M., Duson, B., & King, M. (1982). *Thanatopics: A manual of structured learning experiences for death education.* Kingston, RI: SLE Publications.

Kuiken, D. & Madison, G. (1987–1988). The effects of death contemplation on meaning and purpose in life. *Omega, 18*(2), 103–112.

Lawrence, C. (1987). An integrated spiritual and psychological growth model in the treatment of narcissism. *Journal of Psychology and Theology, 15*(3), 205–213.

Leech, K. (1977). *Soul friend.* New York: Harper & Row.

Lief, J. L. (1986). Compassion and healing encounter. In F. Wald (Ed.), *In quest of the spiritual component of care for the terminally ill: Proceedings of a colloquium* (pp. 121–128). Branford, CT: Yale University School of Nursing.

Lindemann, E. (1979). *Beyond grief: Studies in crisis intervention.* New York: Jason Aranson.

Maddison, D., & Raphael, B. (1975). Conjugal bereavement. In B. Schoenberg, I. Gerber, A. Wiener, A. Kutscher, D. Peretz, & A. Carr (Eds.), *Bereavement, its psychosocial aspects* (pp. 26–40). New York: Columbia University Press.

McCherry, E. (1983). The spiritual dimension of elder health care. *Journal of the Western Society of Gerontology, 8,* 18–21.

Miller, D.L. (1981). *The new polytheism.* Dallas, TX: Spring Publications.

Murphy, M. (1985). The grief process and becoming one's own person. *Studies in The Formative Spirituality, 6*(3), 379–385.

Neumann, E. (1989). Stages of religious experience and the path of depth psychology. *Quadrant, 21*(1), 11–32.

Noy, P. (1984). The three components of empathy: Normal and pathological development. In J. Lichtenberg, M. Bornstein, & D. Silver (Eds.), *Empathy.* Hillside, NJ: Lawrence Erlbaum Associates.

Oates, W. (1982). Forms of grief. In F. Dougherty (Ed.), *The meaning of human suffering.* New York: Human Sciences Press.

Olin, H. S. & Olin, G. B. (1975). Bereavement: An opportunity for emotional growth. In P. Bane, A. Kutscher, R. Neale, & R. Reeves (Eds.), *Death and the ministry: Pastoral care of the dying and bereaved.* (pp. 88–91). New York: Seabury Press.

O'Neil, M. K., Lancee, W. J., & Freeman, S. J. (1987). Loss and depression: A controversial link. *Journal of Nervous and Mental Disease, 175*(6), 354–359.

Osterweis, M., (1985). Bereavement and the elderly. *Aging, 348,* 8–14.

Parkes, C. M. (1970). "Seeking" and "finding" a lost object: Evidence from recent studies of the reaction to bereavement. *Social Science and Medicine, 4,* 187–201.

Parkes, C. M. (1987). Models of bereavement care. *Death Studies, 11*(4), 257–261.

Preston, C. F. (1980). The clergy as bereavement counselors. In B. M. Schoenberg (Ed.), *Bereavement counseling: A multidisciplinary handbook* (pp. 183–194). Westport, CT: Greenwood Press.

Propst, L. R. (1988). *Psychotherapy in a religious framework.* New York: Human Sciences Press.

Rando, T. A. (1986). A comprehensive analysis of anticipatory grief: Perspective, processes, promises, and problems. In T. A. Rando (Ed.), *Loss and anticipatory grief* (pp. 3–38). Lexington, MA: Lexington Books.

Remondet, J. H. (1987). Assessing a widow's grief: A short index. *Journal of Gerontological Nursing, 13*(4), 30–34.

Ronglie, C. (1988). Long-term effects of participation in the bereavement support group at the Hospice of Petaluma. *The American Journal of Hospice Care, 5*(6), 26–29.

Schleifer, S. J., Keller, S. E., & Stein, M. (1987). Conjugal bereavement and immunity. *Israel Journal of Psychiatry and Related Sciences, 24*(1–2), 111–123.

Schmitt, R.F. (1981). Suffering and wisdom. *Journal of Religion and Health, 20,* 108–123.

Sekaer, C. & Katz, S. (1986). On the concept of mourning in childhood. *Psychoanalytic Study of the Child, 41,* 287–314.

Simpson, M. (1987). *Dying, death, and grief: A critical bibliography.* Pittsburgh: University of Pittsburgh Press.

Sklar, F. (1987–1988). Bereavement, ministerial attitudes, and the future of church-sponsored bereavement support groups. *Omega: Journal of Death and Dying, 18*(2), 89–102.

Stevens, M. J., Pfost, K. S. & Wessels, A. B. (1987). The relationship of purpose in life to coping strategies and time since the death of a significant other. *Journal of Counseling and Development, 65*(8), 424–426.

Tate, P. E., & Ward, M. (1987). When a student dies: Helping teachers who grieve. *Education of the Handicapped, 18*(4), 151–156.

Theorell, T., Haggmark, C., & Eneroth, P. (1987). Psycho-endocrinological reactions in female relatives of cancer patients. *Acta Oncologica, 26,* 419–424.

Tillich, P. (1952). *The courage to be.* New Haven, CT: Yale University Press.

Vachon, M. L. S. (1976). Grief and bereavement following the death of a spouse. *Canadian Psychiatric Association Journal, 21,* 35–44.

Wahl, C. W. (1958). The fear of death. *Bulletin of the Menniger Clinic, 12,* 214–223.

Walker, J. I. (1981). *Clinical psychiatry in primary care.* Menlo Park, CA: Addison-Wesley.

Wicks, R. J. (1988). Clarity and obscurity: Critical thinking and cognitive therapeutic principles in the service of spiritual discernment. *Thought, 63,* 77–85.

Worden, J. W. (1976). *Personal death awareness.* Englewood Cliffs, NJ: Prentice-Hall.

Wuthnow, R., Christiano, K., & Kuzlowski, J. (1980). Religion and bereavement: A conceptual framework. *Journal of Social Science amd Religion, 19,* 408–422.

Zisook, S. (1984). Measuring acute grief. *Psychiatric Medicine, 2*(2), 169–176.

Zisook, S., & Shuchter, S. (1985). Time course of spousal bereavement. *General Hospital Psychiatry, 7,* 95–100.

Zisook, S., Shuchter, S. R., & Lyons, L. E. (1987). Predictors of psychological reactions during the early stage of widowhood. *Psychiatric Clinics of North America, 10,* 355–368.

Author Index

Subject Index

About the Author

Richard A. Dershimer (Ed.D., Harvard University) of Charlottesville, VA is currently a private consultant and trainer on matters of grief and bereavement to hospices, school districts, developmental centers, and religious organizations. He has been a Unitarian-Universalist since 1972. For six years he was Director of Education to the Caring Coalition Hospice (now the Hospice of Central New York) in Syracuse, New York. He has been President of the New York State Hospice Association and Adjunct Professor at both Syracuse University and the New School for Social Research. He has published in *The Hospice Journal* and *The American Journal of Hospice Care,* and presented papers at annual meetings of The National Hospice Organization and the New York State Hospice Association.

Before becoming active in the hospice field he enjoyed two distinct careers: as family therapist in the Murray Bowen tradition and as public school teacher, administrator, professor, and for ten years the Executive Officer of the American Educational Research Association in Washington, D.C. In those days he authored *The Federal Government and Educational R & D* and several chapters and articles.

Mark Scrivani (M.A., Syacuse University), who assisted on Part II of this book, is a therapist specializing in grief and loss issues both in private practice and on the staff of the Children's Psychiatric Outpatient Department at St. Joseph's Hospital, Syracuse, New York. He is consulted on matters of bereavement by a wide range of organizations. For several years he has facilitated a support group, "Hope for Youth." He is author of *Love, Mark,* a document for young people facing serious losses.

Psychology Practitioner Guidebooks

Editors

Arnold P. Goldstein, Syracuse University
Leonard Krasner, Stanford University & SUNY at Stony Brook
Sol L. Garfield, Washington University in St. Louis